Praise for *Between the Listening and the Telling:*
How Stories Can Save Us

"In an era of self-serving stories, from car commercials to political brands, it's easy to get cynical about narrative. But in *Between the Listening and the Telling*, Mark Yaconelli ushers us into rooms full of authentic stories, where facades fall and suffering and joy are metabolized. This is an immersive, elegant meditation, an offering of grace."
—Kirsten Powers, CNN senior political analyst and the *New York Times*–bestselling author of *Saving Grace: Speak Your Truth, Stay Centered, and Learn to Coexist with People Who Drive You Nuts*

"Many people can describe what they observe on the surface. Mark Yaconelli is one of those rare human beings who sees all the way into the deeper places—and rarer still, one who can find words to help our hearts grab hold of what is waiting there for us. During days when we can so easily drift from one another and from our better angels, he reminds us how we find our way home. For a world so afflicted with isolation and disconnection, this beautiful book is medicinal."
—John Pavlovitz, author of *If God Is Love, Don't Be a Jerk*

"Mark Yaconelli shows how our stories can form bridges to greater understanding and compassion. *Between the Listening and the Telling* will give you renewed hope and inspiration for how storytelling can bring people closer together. I highly recommend this book to anyone doing community work or leading organizations."
—Mandy Yeahpau, director of social media, IllumiNative

"I have spent my life around stories and storytellers, and Mark Yaconelli captures the vibrancy and necessity of the storytelling world. The beauty of this book lies in its perception, its acuity, its warmth, and its authenticity."
—Lisa Consiglio, CEO and cofounder of Narrative 4

"Scientists, artists, mathematicians, wanderers, dreamers, and the rest of us have been searching for meaning. Mark Yaconelli finds the answer in the heart of the one democracy that we all share—our stories. A lot of things can be taken from us—our houses, our bank accounts, even our lives—but Yaconelli recognizes that nothing can take away the power of storytelling."

—Colum McCann, National Book Award winner
for *Let the Great World Spin*

"*Between the Listening and the Telling* is vulnerable and moving, humorous and humble, beautiful and wise. Story by story, Mark Yaconelli reveals the ancient path that leads to greater love, hope, connection. If you're wondering in this time of alienation and divisiveness whether we still have a common humanity, then this book is for you."

—Melissa Wiginton, vice president for Education Beyond
the Walls, Austin Presbyterian Theological Seminary

"Beautiful, inspiring, timely. Yaconelli invites vulnerability by being vulnerable, courage by being courageous, tears by revealing heartfelt truths, and laughter by being damn funny."

—Max Gimbel, director of the Ford Institute for
Community Building, The Ford Family Foundation

"What a gift Mark Yaconelli has given us! *Between the Listening and the Telling* does more than tell about the goodness of stories; it shows us how our stories can make sense of difficult and joyous experiences, how stories can remove the separations between 'us' and 'them.' We can heal this world through stories. Mark Yaconelli shows us the way."

—Tim Shapiro, director of the Indianapolis
Center for Congregations

Between the Listening and the Telling

BETWEEN the LISTENING and the TELLING

HOW STORIES CAN SAVE US

MARK YACONELLI

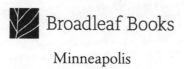

Broadleaf Books

Minneapolis

*To all the brave souls who have told me
their stories, and all the brave souls
who have listened to mine*

"Everything is held together with stories," he thought. *"That is all that is holding us together, stories and compassion."*

—Barry Lopez, *Winter Count*

CONTENTS

M ark Yaconelli is an unusual person, as brilliant as he is plainspoken. He is an activist and a homebody, a contemplative and a goofball, gentle in spirit and charismatic, funny, deeply articulate, and capable of both wonderful compassion and silliness. And he brings all these qualities to his new book.

I cannot imagine there will ever be a more critical need for a book such as this than now. It is an exploration of storytelling as a path to the strength and vulnerability and connection we will so desperately need to survive and come through these times. It is a profound reflection on storytelling as the path to community identity and renewal, for towns and cities and families who have experienced devastation. It is an account of his work teaching people how to make this transformative process available to others. It is an owner's manual for the soul. It is like no other book I've ever read.

As we struggle with the realities of injustice and inequality, the consequences of the pandemic, and the greatest environmental catastrophe of history, Mark Yaconelli offers personal experiences, practical guidance, and stories of resurrection. In this time, like no other, we long for hope and connection. Yaconelli shows us the psychological, spiritual, and logistical underpinnings of his work as an organizer of community storytelling events. Towns and cities frequently summon him following disaster or humiliation, both long term and immediate. By asking the right questions and listening to the answers, he helps people feel their humanity and worth again when these have been stripped away. He helps people cry and spew and laugh together. (And the laughter is so subversive!) These things heal us.

Here he is in his own words: *"We map our world in story. The world falls apart. We map a new world. Again and again we story our lives in order to situate ourselves: I am here, not there. I am here and long to go there. Once found, new possibilities emerge. Curiosity rises within us. We feel the pull to discover new countries, traverse new oceans."*

How do we even begin this process of transformation when we feel crushed and overwhelmed, totally lost or existentially lonely? We show up. Mark has been convincing (and tricking) people into showing up to his workshops and retreats for decades. Twenty years ago, I witnessed him at an evening workshop in which he got several dozen adults and teenagers to stand up, mill around, and bump into each other while muttering, "Mill, mill, mill." I milled—which is SO not me—and came to know the secret, intimate places that my bumpees loved most in the world. And I told them mine. I have since taken that exercise along with me to dubious Sunday school classes and skeptical writing workshops, with great success, laughter, occasional tears, and new friendships.

Through his work, Mark helps people begin to know themselves and their common values. He understands and teaches the great lesson: if people are going to be transformed, it has to come from love, from speaking to one another about the truth of what we have lived. Through the experiences and unique teaching ability he writes about so eloquently in this book, Mark shares the ways in which this truth-telling and trust become possible.

Storytelling is truly an art, and Mark makes it available to all. No one has asked most people to tell their stories in depth—what it was like growing up as the child of an alcoholic or a refugee or a police officer. No one has asked most people where they hid as a child or when their parent could really see them. Telling our stories to someone who is really listening offers us the experience of being seen, of being felt—as in, I feel you. I feel your heart. Can you feel mine? Can you feel the warmth of my caring?

Now more than ever, as we struggle out of deep fear and isolation, we need a teacher and a book such as this. Anyone who works with groups of people who are hurting or seeking in neighborhoods or colleges, churches or prisons, migrant camps or struggling organizations will be shown how story can become a source of sustenance and healing. Writer

Colum McCann says that storytelling is the great democracy, and Mark teaches us how we might be citizens of this beautiful concept. He shows us how to leave the silos of our own points of view, the two-dimensional stuckness of our analytical prisons, and enter into the shared human experiences of connection. Anger and laughter shared, fear and joy passed back and forth—this builds compassion, and this decreases our loneliness. We can breathe differently, because sharing and listening bring expansion and even, in Mark's telling, wonder and homecoming. And these bring hope. Over and over in this book, you will see people move from fear and powerlessness to strength and renewal. You will see people feeling doomed and misunderstood experience those first glimmers of belief in each other, in life, and (hardest of all) in themselves again.

Mark teaches us how and why storytelling has been the collagen of communities since someone in the first cave communities invited others to come sit by the fire, under the moon, and listen to their shared stories. (Almost all humans prefer stories about themselves. I know I do.) It is through this communion—between the listening and the telling, letting ourselves be seen and heard and acknowledged—that we come to the great, longed-for understanding of why we are here, who we are, what really matters, and that we, in fact, matter. This is the ultimate liberation.

This book is a joyful compass toward both freedom and unity. If this is too hard to imagine, just turn the page and begin the journey yourself. You'll find a mesmerizing tour guide in Mark Yaconelli. And be sure to buckle up: finding your way home can be a wild ride, one you may have waited a lifetime to begin.

—Anne Lamott, *New York Times–*
bestselling author of *Help Thanks Wow,*
Bird by Bird, and *Dusk Night Dawn*

1

A PLACE THE SOUL ONCE KNEW

There are moments, often unexpected, when you find yourself at home in your own life. Simple, gentle, ordinary moments. Standing at the kitchen window. Rain outside. The earth springing into green and yellow. The birds, the ridiculous birds, singing without worry beneath the gray sky. For some reason, without effort, the anxiety lifts, your chest relaxes, your senses awaken, a quiet descends, and you are home.

It is in moments like this when I can feel how distant I have been from the life I long to live. I have been homesick and didn't know it. I have been living miles away from my deepest yearnings and not known it. I have been hurrying through my days isolated, fragmented, caught within the jet stream of the anxious world. Only now in the waking stupor do I feel the alienation and loss and, like a sobering drunk, ask, "How long was I out?"

"Months," is the reply. Other times, "Years."

I used to sometimes sense in conversations with friends, in the movies, books, and stories we consumed, an unspoken longing for some kind of great disruption. A disaster. An upheaval. Some systemic breakdown. Cell towers toppled. The internet shorted out. Highways blocked. The human world forced to stop.

It was a fantasy, of course, but one that revealed a kind of helpless despair at the lives we find ourselves compelled to live. It came from an unconscious understanding that our way of life was destructive and unsustainable, dishonest and unsatisfying. A longing for a reckoning and repentance. A longing for limits, for an adult in the room to say, "That is enough." It was a longing for someone to end the tyranny of our every impulse. A longing that we might come to our senses, to our neighbors, to our own basic needs and gifts.

And then the world stopped. The pandemic hit, and we were effectively put under house arrest. Masked and hand-sanitized, we peered with suspicion behind locked doors at the mail carrier, the old couple walking their dog far too casually, our own mother returning a casserole dish. "Step back, Mother. Do not touch the doorknob. Just leave it on the doorstep, Mother!"

The Grim Reaper chillingly made its way through the human population, compelling all of us to not only withdraw from public spaces but also to reflect inwardly: What is the meaning of life? What matters? Why am I living this way? Why have I wasted so much time?

The pandemic ushered us into a liminal space—a disorienting, perilous state of unknowing where we had to confront our relationship to self, others, technology, the past, the earth, the Sacred. A period when everything unhealed within us was dredged to the surface, and it became unquestionably clear that the old stories of mindless consumerism, environmental exploitation, economic inequality, whitebody supremacy were killing us.

Like a rite of passage or a well-crafted story, the pandemic carried us into a state of "disorder," which all wisdom traditions believe is a necessary stage for transformation. Order. Disorder. Reorder. The gift of this disruption has been the uncovering of our fundamental cravings for one another, for the natural world, for family, for rest, for healing, for reconciling the divisions the old stories have kept alive.

Several years ago, I spent six months living and working in northern Wales. It is a rural, ancient land, layered in stories and history. The Welsh people have struggled and suffered to keep their language and, through that language, a connection to the past, to their ancestors, to the land itself. Within that language there is a sacred Welsh word—a word, the Welsh tell me, that doesn't quite translate into English. The word is *hiraeth*. A wise friend from that land once told me the word refers to a particular kind of longing. "What kind of longing?" I asked. He paused, trying to find the words. "A longing for a place or time that the soul once knew."

My son Noah was living in London. He was studying acting, living in an apartment with a handful of American students from across the United States. I called and asked how he was getting along with his roommates. He told me it wasn't easy to connect to the other students because they spent much of their time by themselves, on their phones, on social media. When they did socialize with one another, it often involved heavy drinking. Then he said, "They are all full of longing, but they don't know what they're longing for. They don't even know they're longing."

He could have been describing most of us in the West. Overwhelmed, estranged from our lives, out of touch with our inner vitality, we often find ourselves entranced by activities we know are empty and damaging. We are longing but don't know why. We are yearning for a life we once knew, but we can't seem to remember where we left it.

Two weeks later I called Noah and asked how it was going. He told me he had invited his roommates to go with him to a farmers market. Together they bought chicken and vegetables, apples, lemons, and fresh herbs. They spent the rest of the day cooking: a fall soup, garlic potatoes, beet salad, roast chicken with rosemary and lemon. Apples baked in butter and cinnamon.

Eager to share the feast they had made, Noah and his roommates called the students from the apartment next door and invited them over. They lit candles, gathered leaves and flowers for the table. When the guests arrived, Noah asked everyone to set their phones aside. "We took our time," he told me. "We sat at the table for hours just talking, telling stories about our families, the towns we grew up in, our hopes for the future." He paused. "We sat late into the night, until early morning, just talking. Everyone was so tired, but no one wanted to leave."

Although he didn't say it, my guess is that around that table, the longing momentarily ceased. The emptiness filled. The anxiety calmed. Within those hours rich with story and laughter and human warmth, eight university students found home.

What does it mean to be human? How are we to spend our days? How do we face the troubles of this world? How do we address the heartache for the life we're meant to live but can't remember how? How do we find the place that the soul once knew?

In another time, in another setting, sitting together around a table and sharing stories was as necessary to human life as bread and water. Storytelling was our source of identity, connecting us to our passions, our daily work, the people we encountered, the land we inhabited. Sharing stories was a kind of communion, a shared meal, inviting others to be nourished by what we had lived, suffered, and overcome. Telling stories kept our core values vibrant and accessible, drew to the surface our most generous and courageous qualities. Sitting with friends, long into the evening, trading stories back and forth—this was how we cultivated the wonder of living and the pleasure of human companionship. Sharing our experiences face-to-face gave our lives—no matter how mundane—a sense of value and worth.

We are relational beings. We need others in order to become ourselves. We need relationship to access the deepest gifts of our humanity. We need relationships to live lives that are productive, loving, and meaningful. Sharing stories is how we make a home within ourselves and one another. Story is how we put together the broken pieces. Story is how we identify and heal the suffering within and among us. The practice of storytelling, particularly when sharing the real stories from our own living, tethers us to what matters most—our families, our friends, nature, the hearts we carry, the wondrous mystery of life itself.

Every human being longs for a good question and a listening ear. Where did you like to hide as a child? When was a time you felt deeply betrayed? Where was the place that most felt like home? Who was the love that got away? How did you find yourself in this town? When was the last time you felt truly alive?

———

When my brother Trent's best friend, Eric, died in a military helicopter accident at age twenty, my father asked him to gather Eric's friends at our home. My father was a volunteer pastor, what he jokingly called a "K-Mart pastor" since he'd never been to seminary. But he was a good communicator and well-loved in our small town. So when there was a death, either among the little congregation that he served or among people in town who had no religious affiliation, he was often the one asked to do the funeral.

I had attended a few funerals led by my dad but had never watched his process. That wintry February evening, in a room full of hurting, disoriented young adults, I watched my dad draw out stories from each of us. "Tell me a story about Eric." "Did you and Eric ever get into trouble?" "What was he like when he had a crush on a girl?" "What did he do that annoyed you?" "Tell me a memory of Eric that makes you laugh."

The writer Isak Dinesen once said, "All sorrows can be borne if you put them into a story or tell a story about them." That evening as we told stories that made us laugh, cry, or go silent in wonder, the grief and heartache found release. Over time, the stories we crafted that evening, the stories that my father retold at the funeral, became meeting places where Eric could be encountered—his life felt, his gifts received, his friendship still present.

A few years later, Robert, the brother of a good friend of mine, passed away suddenly. I was in my late twenties and working as a youth minister at a Presbyterian church. My friend Harold called and asked if I would do the funeral. I had no experience officiating a funeral or any public gathering of any significance, but how could I refuse my friend? I called my dad and asked him what to do.

Since he was a minister, I assumed he would offer me a sermon outline. But my dad also knew that most sermons, particularly in a time of grief, can be alienating and abstract. His advice was to gather the stories. "Tell the stories that help people feel Robert's life," he told me. "Get people together. Ask good questions that help them remember and form stories about their life with him. Draw out the memories and then listen and take notes on the stories they tell. That's what's needed. Any meaning, any hope, any truths that need to be spoken will come from there."

Without having to wait for a funeral, how do we make contact with the power of the stories we embody, the stories planted within us, the life-giving stories that dwell between us? How can we access story in ways that are sacred and purposeful? The space matters. The listening matters. The telling matters. It matters where you are, who is in the room, the place in your heart from which the story is told.

One year into the pandemic, the brand-new Phoenix High School has opened for in-person classes. Many of the students enrolled in this small southern Oregon school are traumatized. Not only because of coronavirus anxiety and social isolation, but also because six months earlier the Almeda wildfire burned much of the region to the ground. More than 3,500 homes and businesses were destroyed, and approximately 5,000 people were displaced.

After disinfecting our hands and signing the requisite contact tracing form, my colleague Erica and I are escorted to Mr. Rodreick's classroom. His afternoon class is titled

"How to Become a Better Human Being." The classroom is watched over by large profile posters of American saints: Martin Luther King Jr., Cesar Chavez, Helen Keller, Rosa Parks, Abraham Lincoln. Erica and I stand self-consciously in front of the nine students, who look like enormous cockatoos in their white-beaked breathing masks.

We have been asked by the Oregon Health Authority to help students share stories as a way to reduce anxiety and depression. In *My Grandmother's Hands*, therapist and author Resmaa Menakem depicts trauma as "a wordless story our body tells itself about what is safe and what is a threat." The work, according to Menakem, is to "metabolize our pain." Sitting in circles, listening compassionately to one another, is one way we can digest our suffering and activate our capacity to heal.

I diagram a few story patterns on the white board. I talk about how most stories present a conflict, a problem, a difficulty. This has been a year of immense difficulty. We ask the students to write a personal story about a struggle they have faced this past year: *Describe life before and during the struggle. Where are you in the story now?*

The teacher passes out materials. The students go inward. The quiet scratching of pens on paper feels intimate. After ten minutes, we sit in a large circle and the students read what they've written. They are stories of loss, of isolation, self-judgment, unending worry. Of carrying the pain of their parents. When the sharing ends, we ask, "What was it like to exchange stories?" A broad-shouldered youth with a Seattle Seahawks jersey raises his hand. "Joyful," he says.

"Joyful?" I repeat, somewhat surprised.

"Yeah. Even though everyone's depressed, I could feel myself in each person's story. And that's joyful."

This is how stories can save us. We step into the reality of another person's existence and instead of judgment feel kinship. When we say, "Tell me your story," we're really asking, "Can I relive your experience with you? Can I try and see as you have seen, feel as you have felt, know the world as you have known it?" The honest listening and telling of personal experiences naturally endears us to one another. The illusion of separateness dissipates, and we see ourselves in one another's story. When that happens, we are no longer able to demonize, ridicule, oppress, or neglect the other. This is not rocket science. This capacity is a natural, hardwired, human inclination that anyone can engage. And when we do, we can heal our families, our world, ourselves.

One afternoon, sitting by the stone fireplace in a farmhouse just outside the Welsh-speaking town of Bala, I listen as seventy-two-year-old Dorothi Madogwen Evans tells her granddaughter about the house we are in. "This hearth was built by your great-great-grandfather. He made it by hand using stones he hauled up from the little creek just down the way. Your grandfather was raised in this home, and when he grew up he built this kitchen and your parents' bedroom.

Do you see those beams overhead? They are from the trees he cut on this land. Your grandfather lived here too when he was little, just like you. And when he grew up, we moved into this house."

She pauses, then continues. "We raised your mother in this home. She used to play hide-and-seek down in the basement, just like you do. We added the upstairs bedrooms for your mother and her brothers also using wood from the trees on this land. And now you and your brothers sleep in those same rooms and help with the lambing just as your mother did. Just as your grandfather did when he was your age."

Sitting there that afternoon, I basked in the light of Dorothi's stories, warming myself by the fire as she passed on to her granddaughter the stories she had gathered from her life. Like rich and nourishing food, Dorothi told story after story, feeding her granddaughter history, identity, and connection to the past, her relatives, the land, her own origin. I watched as the young girl's soul gathered in her grandmother's words and presence.

These stories will be the roots of a meaningful life. These stories will become a home no matter where the young girl's life leads. Even if she grows up and moves to New York City to become a stockbroker, she will always carry that sense of relationship, that sense of home. She will carry that knowledge through the stories she has been told, through the stories she has lived, through the stories she tends within her. One day she may fall in love, and in the intimacy of that relationship share her story, her identity, the heart of who she is. "When I was a little girl, I lived in a farmhouse built by my great-grandfather in the North of Wales. . . ."

Where are the hearths, the dinner tables, the kitchens where we are invited to share the stories that come from the root of our living? When will someone invite us to share the stories that connect us to what matters most? The stories that bring deep laughter? The stories that dissipate the loneliness? The stories that excavate and heal the injustices we've suffered? The stories that give our lives meaning and purpose? The stories that raise within us a quiet gratitude at the painful wonder of it all?

———

This book is a reflection on the nature of stories within our individual and collective lives. The writing is based on decades of working with individuals, communities, and their lived stories. I've spent thousands of hours listening to people as they sifted through the chaotic laundry of their lives, working to make meaning, struggling to express their stories. In my work with The Hearth nonprofit, I help people tell stories in order to find acceptance, grieve loss, deepen friendships, strengthen families, shed light on an injustice, dispel an oppressive stereotype, celebrate the wonder of being alive. I've sat and listened to health-care workers, combat veterans, environmental scientists, abuse survivors, refugees, farmers, educators, stay-at-home parents, college students, the terminally ill, faith leaders, incarcerated people, social justice activists—people from all walks of life with diverse economic, social, racial, and ethnic backgrounds.

For years I did this work solely for The Hearth—drawing out stories, creating spaces for people to narrate what they'd lived. And then word spread and I began to get calls from outside my community. Combat veterans asking for help in sharing stories no one wanted them to tell. A youth shelter hoping I could draw forth stories from the LGBTQ community. A graduate school looking to create a space where people of color could exchange stories about their experiences of race. A hospice doctor asking for help communicating stories of death and grief. A city manager needing stories to soothe political tensions. An environmentalist seeking to gather stories to preserve an estuary.

In all my careful listening, I've observed how speaking our stories can liberate us individually and collectively—at times transforming residents into neighbors, enemies into friends, and towns into communities. In doing this work, it has become apparent to me that the power of story is the power of *relationships*. In other words, giving testament to our experience generates meaning when it connects us to people, the earth, the sacred, our pasts, our own inner gifts and wounds. Through this work I've come to believe that all human divisions, both within and between us, can begin to be healed through listening and sharing stories.

This book seeks to share some of the ways I've witnessed healing take place. In a disconnected age, an age of runaway loneliness, I believe it is story that can transform us. Each chapter offers reflections on our private and public relationships. Chapters 1 through 3 focus more on the individual and the way we become estranged or empowered by the stories we carry. The later chapters tend to focus more on our shared lives and the way story can connect, engage, inspire, and mobilize for the common good. Throughout the book there are story "interludes" that offer a respite from the discussion of stories. These interludes—true stories from my own network of relationships—function like pieces of music, inviting the reader to feel the meaning of the preceding chapters without having to define it.

Ultimately this book is about the soul of storytelling and the recovery of that natural, accessible, medicinal power that waits within every person, within every community. Every life holds beauty. Every life encounters suffering. Every life is a struggle to claim dignity and worth. And each of us has lived a story worth telling.

2

CONFESSION

Sometimes on long walks with my teenage daughter, she will say, "I want to hear a story from your childhood." I usually react by making a joke or asking her a question or distracting her with some observation of the world. To share some childhood episode from my life is more than a transfer of information and ideas. To tell stories from my childhood is to relive those moments. To tell the story of my childhood to my daughter is to ask her to relive it with me, and there are many moments from childhood I don't want to relive.

Storytelling is the most intimate form of communication. It's a way of inviting the listener to enter into what we have known, what we have suffered, what we have overcome. When we listen well to another's story, it blooms within the body, creating an intimate connection between teller and listener—heart races, eyes well with tears, the belly shakes with laughter. And when we share something we have lived, a joy or suffering from our own lives, the listener is invited into our very being: to see what we have seen, hear what we have heard, touch and feel what we have known. In this way, storytelling is a sacred transaction. The stories of our lives are an offering, a kind of confession, an intimate revelation. And when they are received, we find the story has become a tether, binding us to one another.

▬▬▬▬

When I was fourteen years old, I attended a three-week-long summer camp in the Sierra Nevada mountains just outside of Yosemite. The camp was full of summer leisure— long afternoons spent sunbathing and swimming, day hikes up into the mountains, Capture the Flag, skit nights, crafts, square dancing, and sing-alongs by the campfire. It was also a Christian camp. We spent some portion of every morning by ourselves in silence, reading the Bible, praying, and journaling. We had what were called "cabin devotionals," in which we reflected in groups about our lives and talked about basic Christian stories and values. Each night one of the counselors would give a talk, often a testimonial about their own experience of the Christian faith.

I am acutely aware of the destructive, hurtful, or just plain deadening aspects of the Christian religion. I have listened to the painful stories of many friends and some family members about the way the Christian faith twisted their sense of self and the world, promoted hatred and judgment toward others, filled them with loathing toward their own human impulses, blinded them to basic truths, or simply wasted their time with meaningless words and hypocritical teachings. This was not my experience. I grew up, for the most part, with a healthy, life-giving experience of the Christian faith—a faith that enlarged my compassion, gave me a sense of worth despite suffering, and provided me with a source of love and meaning. My father (who was also my pastor growing up), the people who went to our church, the counselors at the summer camp were funny, vulnerable, passionate, creative, loving people. And they drew these qualities out in me.

On one of the final days of the last summer I attended camp, the dean asked if I would give my testimony at the closing campfire. He encouraged me to tell the story of my life as honestly as I could, including any doubts, struggles, or questions I had about the Christian faith. I remember spending the afternoon walking through the woods, trying to compose some sort of talk to give at the campfire.

It had been a very painful year. My father, in what amounted to a public scandal for our small town, had left the church where he was a volunteer pastor, divorced my mother, and moved in with his secretary. My mother, in the throes of mental illness, had recently been hospitalized after spending weeks driving haphazardly across the United States, believing she was being pursued by the FBI.

I had no idea how to talk about any of this. I didn't know how to tell a story about the mixed admiration and resentment I felt toward my father, the shame and concern I felt toward my mother. I did not know how to order this experience—how to extract the hurt and anxiety and shape it into a story. I had never heard anyone talk about mental illness, divorce, adultery. I needed someone to listen to me, to ask honest questions, to help me arrange the confused, broken pieces of my adolescent life.

The night of my testimony we met on a rocky outcropping that looked over the treed mountains. High up in that remote valley, the stars felt as close as fireflies. Songs were sung and then I was invited to come up and share my story. I stood in front of the great orange bonfire, a shadowed outline in front of my peers, and tried to put my life into story. But I had no words, no understanding, no story to tell. I stood suffering in silence and then, finally, lowered my head and wept.

"There is no greater agony than bearing an untold story inside of you," Maya Angelou once wrote. For most of my young life, I walked around feeling the agony of an untold story. It wasn't until I went in search of healing that I found the shapes, the patterns, the listening companions to help narrate my life into words.

━━━━

Sharing our stories is a fundamental practice of healing. We can't seem to move forward, can't access our fullhearted passions, until we first sew our experiences together into story: This is what happened. These are the chain of events that led me to now. This is how I learned to find love. This is how I survived abuse. This is how I trace the origin of fear. Once upon a time I was at point A, then suffered B, which sent me to C. Now, thirty years later, I find myself at point D.

A story is a handful of breadcrumbs leading to home. A story is a divining rod and we the subterranean river. A story is a map and we the mapmakers plotting the landscapes of our lives. We need a story to locate ourselves in the world. Without a true story, told from the ground of our own lives, we can often feel lost or, worse, imprisoned by the stories others have constructed for us.

In recovery and support groups, in psychotherapy, in truth and justice work, we use story to trace our wounds, to express our identity, to plot our trajectory, to unearth our collective trauma. We tell a story called *I Have Worth*, a story titled *Meeting the Expectations of Others*, a story named *I Am My Sister's Keeper*, a story called *Hiding*. Telling stories about our lives is how we work out our freedom. To place our lives into story and tell it to others—whether dark or hopeful— makes healing possible.

—————

When I was twenty-six, I entered a graduate training pro- gram for spiritual directors. For four years, I had been studying and practicing various spiritual disciplines that immersed me in silence, prayer, and meditation. These prac- tices calmed my anxiety, tended my wounds, and helped me become more present to my life. In monasteries, retreat centers, and meditation groups, I was beginning to find the space I needed to trace the storylines of my own life.

Spiritual direction comes out of the Christian tradition and involves developing the sensibilities and skills for listening contemplatively and compassionately to the soul struggle of another person. Through training in the art of spiritual direction, I hoped to experience and embody the power of companionship in the spiritual journey.

On the first day of the training, participants were placed in groups of six and told that each person would get forty-five minutes to tell their life story. As each of us walked to our assigned rooms, I looked around anxiously. There were so many interesting people, so many people who looked like they had an exciting story to tell. I remember a young woman with long brown hair, colorful beads, a guitar, and a hippie-styled leather fringe vest. There was a ponytailed man with cutoff sleeves and shoulder tattoos of red and green Mexican saints. Standing near the coffee table, a bearded man in a red scarf talked about his travels through eastern Europe searching for the Black Madonna.

Disappointingly, none of these colorful characters were assigned to my life story group. As I took my seat, I surveyed the other group members and sighed: a retired pastor, an elderly socialite from Newark, a fifty-something professor of social ethics, a middle-aged homemaker, an English teacher from Florida dressed in golf pants and polo shirt. Even though there seemed to be some racial and economic diversity, this had to be a collection of the least interesting people in the program.

I stood and walked out of the room, found one of the retreat leaders, and asked for reassignment. "I'm just so much younger than most of the participants," I told him. "I think I'd be more comfortable with others closer to my age." He smiled and explained that this kind of age diversity was intentional. Dejected, I walked by another group's room just as the hippie woman barked, "Anyone uncomfortable with an X-rated story should switch groups." Everyone laughed as the tattooed man replied, "Are you kidding? I paid fifty bucks to get in here!" I couldn't help but feel envious. While the carefree musician was telling her tales of the *Kama Sutra*, I'd be listening to monologues about faculty politics, plugged milk ducts, and the futility of school testing.

I returned to my group and slouched back into my chair as our group facilitator asked, "All right, who would like to start?" The heavily made-up woman from New Jersey raised her hand. "I'll go." I prepared myself for a forty-five-minute tale of museum fundraisers and cocktail parties.

"Do we have to tell our story chronologically?" the woman asked.

"No," the facilitator replied, "You can tell your story however you want."

"All right," the woman said thoughtfully. She paused, gathered herself, and with eyes closed, she began. "Twenty years ago I woke up in a motel in Connecticut. I was naked, lying on the floor in a room filled with empty bottles of vodka and vials of morphine. There were used needles and condoms all over the room, and my body was bruised and

sore. I sat up, showered, dressed, and called the motel manager to ask where I was, what day it was. I had no memory
of the past three days. No idea why I was hours from Newark, so far from my home. No idea who I had been with,
or what had been done to me. I didn't know where my kids
were, where my husband was. I didn't know anything. That
was the first day. The first day I realized I had a problem.
That I needed help."

I was shocked. I had no idea this well-dressed lawyer's
wife could have this kind of recklessness in her. I looked
around at the group expecting to see expressions of disbe-
lief. Instead, I found faces that were present, kind, and full
of empathy. We sat in the silence, the woman's vulnerability
drawing out our compassion. The woman looked around to
see if we were with her. Assured of our presence, she took
a deep breath and let her eyes fill with emotion. Suddenly I
could feel how the group—our presence, our witness—was
drawing the story out. We were traveling companions, journeying with her back in time. In order for her to go back
to that Connecticut motel—in order to tell the story—she
needed us to accompany her.

The woman proceeded to tell a story of a troubled marriage, a prescription drug addiction, a childhood of abuse
and neglect, a gnawing self-hatred, hospitalization, suicide
attempts, a wise friend, a divorce, a struggle to renew her
relationship with her children, a new marriage, a spiritual
awakening, a daily struggle for self-acceptance. The story
ended, and I found myself full of a kind of holy wonder. I

had no idea a woman who looked like this could have such pain, confusion, and bravery inside of her.

We took a break and then regathered. The retired minister went next. He had been born in a remote village in Honduras to parents who were farmers, devout Catholics. He described life on the farm, his relationship with his sister, the pleasure of caring for animals. Then his story took a turn. "I guess I was around twelve years old when I fell in love with a boy. At the time, it felt natural. One day, we were walking through a cornfield and I kissed him— completely ignorant of the taboo. One afternoon, my father saw me holding hands with this boy down by our creek. He was not an angry or violent man, but when he saw me, he stomped down the embankment, grabbed me by the neck, walked me to the house, and beat the hell out of me. I had cracked ribs, my testicles swelled up like grapefruit, my left eye closed shut. My mother had to take me to my grandmother's house. It was months before I recovered."

The retired minister went on to tell of his disconnection from his father and deep sexual repression. At sixteen he left Honduras and migrated across the border into the United States. He lived in immigrant camps, picked fruit, and slept in open fields. Eventually he met a social worker who saw his gifts and helped him go to college and then on to graduate school. Ashamed and terrified of his sexual orientation, he married a woman, raised four kids, and pastored a church for thirty years. At age sixty-four, only a few months before retirement, he felt a deep urge to tell the truth of his identity. He confessed first to his wife and spoke with each of his grown children. "I didn't want a divorce. I just wanted to be truthful about who I was."

The following Sunday, he told his story to his congregation. Other than kissing a boy at age twelve, he had never had any sexual contact with men, yet he felt he could no longer hide his true identity. "For thirty years I had preached to people to tell the truth, that God would love them just as they are. It was time I practiced what I was preaching."

His wife left him. His children stopped speaking to him. His church fired him. He was defrocked by his denomination and lost his retirement benefits. "I now live alone, in a tiny apartment, in a dangerous part of Cincinnati, Ohio," he told us. "I have no work, no income other than social security. A few former church members give me a little money each month to live off of. I am lonely. I miss my wife. I miss my kids. But I'm no longer hiding. No longer pretending."

Again, I was shocked. I would never have guessed that this story, this heartbreak, this suffering lived in a man who looked so, well, ordinary.

Around the circle we went, each person's story full of tragedy, unmet longing, hurt, and forgiveness. Each story unexpected. Each story focused on the struggle to find acceptance, healing, and freedom. Each story arousing compassion in those of us listening.

I was the last one to speak. The poet Mary Oliver once wrote that the soul is made entirely out of attentiveness. Receiving the compassionate attention of others, I felt my soul come to the surface. For the first time, between the listening and the telling, I began to feel and understand the struggle of my own life.

I left that day of life stories feeling wholly disoriented. If this group of plain-faced people was full of such pain and courage, what lived within the lives of my neighbors, my coworkers, the people I passed on the street? Suddenly I was filled with a new sense of curiosity, less judgment, and more empathy for those around me as well as for myself.

From time to time—among friends, over meals with strangers, in small groups, or on long plane rides—I receive the gift of attention. "What's your story?" someone will ask. "How did you get here?" Every time I tell it, it's different. Every time I receive the gift of attention, my soul expands. And every time I finish my story, I discover myself standing in a new land.

The story begins at a dinner table with a son scrambling to keep his father's attention.

It begins in a car driven by a mother who believes she's fleeing the government.

It begins with eating honeycomb stolen from my grandfather's bees.

It begins in tears. It begins in awe.

It begins in a remote cabin walking a baby daughter to sleep with a heart full of grief.

It begins in a snowstorm searching for love.

It begins in a convent.

It begins with a kiss from a beautiful Sardinian chef.

It begins in loss. It begins in hope.

It starts out familiar and then becomes strange and uncertain.

It begins in the middle, loops back, then falls forward into a deep realization.

It begins.

It begins.

We map our world in story. The world falls apart. We map a new world. Again and again we story our lives in order to situate ourselves: I am here, not there. I am here and long to go there. Once found, new possibilities emerge. Curiosity rises within us. We feel the pull to discover new countries, traverse new oceans.

The longer we live, the more we understand our lives not as a single timeline leading to a particular end point, not as Jacob's ladder rising step-by-step toward perfection, but as a landscape: a topography with rivers and forests and deserts and springs and high mountains and vales and all of it undiscovered, all of it unknown, with hidden creatures and monsters and spirits and village folk and folk angels and holy sites and desecrated sites and veins of gold and veins of fool's gold and all of it a terrifying, wondrous mystery.

3

THE CATACOMBS

M y father, in a uniquely American way, was an entre-
preneur, a prankster, a pastor, an editor of a satirical
Christian magazine, a popular speaker, an author, a pub-
lisher of youth ministry books, an owner of a small-town
television store, a host of a weekly local radio show, and a
national Toastmaster champion. In the little town where we
lived, Dad was known primarily as a volunteer pastor of an
unconventional church, a church, he often said, "for people
who don't like church." He was a warm, creative, passionate, energizing, fun father to have around—when he had
time to be around.

Dad spent much of his time when I was growing up
running an irreverent, humorous magazine that mocked
the excesses of the Christian church. Called *The Wittenberg
Door*, the magazine was part of the 1960s zeitgeist lampoon-
ing the Christian establishment and ridiculous excesses
of American evangelical Christianity. There was no lack of
buffoons, from Jimmy Swaggart, to Tammy Faye Bakker,

to Jerry Falwell, to Oral Roberts and his five-hundred-foot Jesus. The magazine was subversive and off-color—so much so that it once ran a cartoon of a pastor standing at a magazine rack, pretending to look at *Playboy* while reading a copy of *The Wittenberg Door* carefully tucked inside the covers. Sections such as "Truth Is Stranger Than Fiction," the Green Weenie Award (often given to pompous, hypocritical Christian celebrities), and articles by *The Door's* make-believe founder, H. Winfield Tutte, made the magazine popular among Christian pastors and seminary students with a sense of humor.

The unconscious message from my father to his kids was to live our lives, to measure our lives, by stories. "Live your life like a great story"—that was the unspoken imperative my dad gave to me. He told and retold stories from books, from his experiences, and from the Bible in fresh and humorous ways, but the teaching was clear: fashion your life similarly, into a story worth remembering. This legacy was both a gift and a curse.

———

Within the catacombs of the soul are sacred paintings, captured memories that hold the emotional truths at the root of our being. Throughout our lives we find ourselves contemplating these layered images in search of greater understanding. Each icon a window into some unique tension we've lived but can't fully integrate.

When asked about our lives, we become a docent within our own inner museum, standing before various exhibits, describing what we see, working to put them in some sort of order that might make sense to others, to ourselves. The arrangement depends on the question and the storyline we're following: betrayals, childhood courage, natural disasters, close calls, sacred objects, adventures in sex, rites of passage, mother, father, home—images are gathered and lined up according to theme.

But when the telling is over, the museum closed, the lights turned off, our memories simply hang silently within the body, often without any arc or purpose, waiting to be rearranged for the next telling.

When I was in my early thirties, the *Wall Street Journal* did a profile of the work I was doing with teenagers. For years I had been studying how to use Christian contemplative practices like silence, solitude, and meditation to invite self-awareness. While at San Francisco Theological Seminary, I received a grant to try out these practices with young people. Hailed as a reform movement within the world of Christian youth formation, the article inspired other national media outlets to report on my endeavors. Almost overnight, I began receiving invitations to speak, teach, write, and lead retreats for faith communities, parent groups, seminaries, and nonprofit organizations across the United States and abroad. When I taught, I relied on stories. And when people came out of silence, solitude, or meditation, they shared stories. I began traveling, speaking, and telling stories.

And all of this was familiar to me.

———

Much of what I know about stories I learned from my dad.

It is 1972. My father and a handful of his colleagues have organized one of the first national conventions for Christian youth workers. I am six years old, sitting at the head table for the final night's banquet. It is mayhem. One table wears balloon animals on their heads. Another group wears oxford shirts tucked into boxers. A small band of youth workers stand on their chairs and play "The Old Rugged Cross" on kazoos. Another table responds by singing "My Ding-A-Ling." At one point a group of youth workers stands up with spoons hanging from the ends of their noses and the whole room breaks into cheers.

As food is brought out, people begin to take the stage delivering inane testimonies to roommates, church secretaries, and Gomer, the Old Testament prophet. The wait-staff, at first bewildered, are soon drawn into the chaos as youth leaders sing to them or bring them on stage to receive impromptu awards.

The lights dim and my father introduces a special guest, the TV evangelist and healer "Ernest Angley." With hair slicked back and large sweat stains under the armpits of his white suit, a friend of my dad's enters the room ranting and spitting into his handheld microphone, impersonating the televange-list. His southern drawl and saccharine preaching incite hoots and hallelujahs from the youth workers. At one point, he calls for silence. Then, as if relaying a telegraph sent directly to his mind, he reports, "I see a boy whose ears are blocked and in need of the Spirit's healing power." This is my cue.

I stand and walk slowly and somberly to the edge of the stage. The crowd is surprised by the sight of a child in their midst. He pulls me up onto the stage, thrusts his face close to mine, and begins sputtering televernacular ravings while I stand perfectly still. At the gibbering crescendo he shouts, "Heeeeeeeeaaaaawwl!" while pressing his hands against my ears. As practiced, I fall backward into the wait-ing arms of his assistants. He pulls me upright and tests my hearing. After wincing and stuttering, I acknowledge his voice and he calls for the crowd to applaud his miraculous power. Right on cue the crowd claps with cries of "Amen, brother!" He releases my arm and charges me to go out and tell the world what God has done. I begin to walk off stage and then, as rehearsed, proceed to bump into chairs and people. Arms outstretched, I feel my way across the stage blindly, as if the miracle worker has crossed his powers and accidently moved the illness from my ears into my eyes. The crowd erupts in laughter as the spotlight follows me bum-bling through the banquet floor, knocking into tables and chairs. I soak it up.

The skits end, plates are cleared, and a lone guitarist stands on the stage leading the group in singing. Then my dad stands to speak. With his full beard and long hair, he looks like Jerry Garcia's younger brother. He is hilarious, animated, irreverent, emotionally moving, and full of stories. His talk ends and I climb up onto the table, clapping as hard as I can.

Ever since I was a young boy, I have always sat in the front row watching, listening, studying. Look through my stored memories and I can show you photograph after photograph of me sitting in the front row at church, camps, conferences, and festivals, trying to absorb my father's gifts—his use of stories, how they moved between speaker and listener, how he drew people into laughter or silence or tears or prayer.

For much of his life, my dad was most available, most present, most himself in front of an audience. I think this is one reason I sat in the front row. Until the last years of his life, Dad was much more vulnerable and open when standing in front of an audience than he was in one-on-one encounters. Listening to him speak, I learned about his story. It was common for him in his preaching and speaking to recall childhood memories, confess his own struggles, unmask his own gifts.

One way to become a storyteller is to have a father who is impatient, busy, easily distracted, whose attention you crave. My dad traveled a lot. He missed birthdays. He missed holidays. He missed childhoods. When you did manage to get time with him, he had the patience of a young adolescent. The question might be "How was school?" or "What did you do this weekend?" As soon as I responded, my dad would start an internal stopwatch. I had two minutes. If I did not have a good opening line, if I spent too much time on setting or context or unnecessary characters, he would start fidgeting, his eyes looking around for something of interest. If I didn't change tack and find a compelling image or plot, he would stand up, pretending to still be listening. He would go through the mail, empty the dishwasher, look through the refrigerator. Over time you learned how to keep his focus, you learned how to speak in compelling sentences and dramatic plotlines. This is how you kept Dad's attention. This is how you garnered his love.

My father loved to tell stories that revealed human imperfection and our need for some kind of larger, healing sense of grace and acceptance. He often told stories that contained radical acts of love. Growing up I was inspired by the images from his talks. They made me want to be a more vulnerable, loving person. But the shadow side of his message was that ordinary life, daily life, the life of children and home and family and day-to-day living was unremarkable, uninteresting. Life experiences that didn't fit the dramatic plotlines my father cherished were discarded on the cutting floor. This is where my siblings and I often lived. This is where my mother lived: in the shadows, on the cutting floor.

Some of the lasting images I carry of my early years with my mother are sad, surreal, terrifying, lonely, full of guilt and shame. My mother was unhappy, frustrated with her life, and often bitter and angry. I usually felt sorry for her and at the same time couldn't wait to get away from her. I have many scenes of my father being away and my mom thrashing about the kitchen, yelling, slamming pots and pans, tipping over the garbage, throwing toys, chairs, books onto the floor or sometimes at us kids. Scenes where my siblings and I hid in bedrooms, in the backyard, in the garage out back.

My dad's speaking trips would sometimes last for two or three weeks or more. Mom was the one left at home. She was the one who cared for us. She cooked the meals, bought our clothes, drove us to school events. The moments when she wasn't enmeshed in her own anger and unhappiness were rare. She did enjoy watching us play sports and participate in school performances. Sometimes she would dance with us when we put on records. One year she subscribed to a classical music series where every month we received a new record highlighting Bach, Beethoven, Mozart, and other famous composers. At times she would buy tickets for us to attend community theater and music performances. Once she took my young sisters on a bike trip (although underprepared and questionably safe) through the San Juan Islands. Every once in a while, she would put out fancy place settings, turn on one of her new classical records, and my three siblings and I would sit with her at the dining table and eat by candlelight. She wanted more connection, more activity, more adventure, more joy in her life, but she didn't know how to get it.

After my father's affair and divorce, my mother began to suffer psychotic breakdowns. This is when she became a "storyteller" of sorts. Unfortunately, she became a delusional one, a storyteller whose stories often involved malevolent figures who snuck into our house at night to rearrange furniture, steal shoes, and gather information for the FBI. My siblings and I did not know how to respond to these stories. So we just listened and then stayed quiet.

According to psychologist Alice Miller, what most adults learn from childhood is "the art of not experiencing feelings." In her research, she found that a child can only fully experience their emotions when they have someone who is present, someone who accepts and understands them. If that doesn't happen, the feelings remain held within the body, often captured within a particular scene or memory, hung within the soul's museum until they can be felt, embodied, storied, and released.

It's 1980, and my brother and I sit with our father at a local hamburger joint for our weekly get together. We are joking around when my father turns serious. Although it has only been a few months or so since the divorce, he tells us he is planning on marrying his young secretary. As we had promised our mom, we tell him we will not be attending the wedding. He stands up and, without saying a word, leaves the restaurant. My brother and I head home assuming Dad will never speak to us again.

How do you get angry at a prankster, someone you admire, someone who makes you laugh, someone who holds some wisdom, someone who can be vulnerable and honest about their faults, someone who is fun? How can you be resentful of someone who is doing good work, someone who has helped so many people, someone who loves you?

It's difficult.

———

I was fifteen years old, living in my father's house. Six months earlier my mother had been placed in the mental ward of a local hospital and diagnosed with schizoaffective disorder. My young sisters, who had spent months enduring my mother's frightening delusions of encroaching federal agents and mafia hitmen, had been recently removed from her home and brought to live with my dad, new stepmom and stepsister, my brother, and me.

One night, sometime around three o'clock in the morning, the phone began to ring in my bedroom. When I finally heard the ringing, I quickly got up, leaned over my brother's bed, and answered it. "Mark? I need to meet you. Can I come pick you up?" It was my mother, in a voice that sounded frightened, secretive, and crazy. I stayed quiet for a moment to think. I was the eldest son. She was no longer my father's responsibility. There was no choice.

While my brother slept, I quietly dressed, made my way upstairs, and waited by the front window, my mind disoriented by the strange hour. In a few minutes I saw the headlights bend in front of the house and my mother's car pull beside the curb. I waited, hoping my father would hear the engine noise, come out from his room, and rescue me—but the house stayed still. I undid the lock and scurried across the lawn, and we drove away.

The car smelled rank with body odor, stale coffee, and drugstore perfume. There were legal papers, plastic bags, fast-food wrappers, and Styrofoam cups piled thick across the car seats and floor. My mother's face was haggard, her body slumped forward, her eyes wary and nervous like a wild animal. She drove in an odd silence. Lost in some inner world, her face shifted through various dark and horrific expressions.

She drove without destination, the car drifting from left to right. Our small, working-class town was still asleep. No traffic, no houselights. From time to time I grabbed the wheel to keep us from crashing, causing her to laugh and smirk, saying, "Geez, you're jumpy!" I both hoped and feared we'd be stopped by the police.

Then she began to speak. "We are in a war. It's everywhere." Her voice was cold, all-knowing. She put her eyes on me, studied my face carefully, and then said, "I think you understand what I'm talking about." I continued to look forward, nervously trying to anticipate an accident. I replied as lightly as I could, "No, I don't know what you're talking about."

"Really? Come on! You don't notice what's going on with the police, the government, the streetlights flickering on and off, your father?" She chuckled and shook her head at the mention of my father.

"I really don't know what you're talking about." I spoke in steady, calm notes, the way you might speak to a gunman. "You seem tired, Mom. It's late. Why don't you get some sleep?"

She erupted into a volume that tore at her vocal cords, "Right! Get some sleep! That will solve everything. Shut her up! She doesn't know what the hell she's talking about!" Mom slammed the steering wheel. I sat shocked and shaking from the violence in her voice, when abruptly, eerily, her emotion suddenly switched. Her body went slack, her face turned uncertain and vulnerable. "I don't know what to do, Mark."

For the next couple of hours my mother drove us up and down the streets of our town, describing the dark conspiracies that gathered around us. The descriptions were intricate and complicated and filled with frightening anecdotes. I tried to make myself as still and silent as possible in hopes she would forget me and stop talking.

My silence had no effect. She became more and more animated, less and less aware that she was driving. Although I did not possess a driver's license, eventually I convinced her to give me the wheel. Sometime early dawn, I drove us to a truck stop diner where I had just enough money to buy two cups of coffee and a side of pancakes. We sat in a booth and I focused on the waitress's face, the sound of truck drivers conversing, the radio playing in the back kitchen, the movement of the busboy as he cleared tables—trying to anchor myself to a reality outside of my mother's.

We sat and ate while my mother made contorted faces, whispering to herself and to imaginary figures. Nauseated by the lack of sleep and the strange breakfast hour, I pushed through the guilt and fear and broke her trance. "I need to get ready for school, Mom." She sobered for a moment and then looked at me with disappointment. "Fine. I don't know if you'll be safe. But if that's what you want . . ."

We drove up to the house, and I exited without saying goodbye. With everyone still sleeping, I sneaked in through the back door, showered, dressed, made my lunch, placed a note on the counter, and then quickly left for school hours early, afraid my mother would call again. I went to my classes, hung out with my girlfriend, joked with friends, attended track practice, and for twenty years said nothing to anyone about what had happened.

The untold stories never go away. The soul, the old restless storyteller within, won't stay quiet. She continues to wander the catacombs, pulling out old photographs, lining them up, narrating forgotten histories, recalling lost feelings we thought we had smothered. Patiently, persistently, the soul waits for us to give her our full attention. Waits for us to feel the ungrieved grief, the overwhelming fear, the hidden anger, the repressed joy, the acceptance of what we know is true.

I managed for a long time to hide my mother's illness from my closest friends, from extended family, from myself. Twenty years of phone calls from my mother from undisclosed locations, asking if I was safe, telling me she was on the run. Twenty years of unannounced visits from my mother, often in the middle of the night, after spending weeks living in her car, sometimes driving for days with hardly any sleep or food. Twenty years of listening to my mother in locked bathrooms, in closed bedrooms, over phone lines holding strange and angry conversations with imaginary figures—her voice low and gravely one moment, high pitched and childlike the next. Twenty years of my siblings, my wife, my children on high alert, afraid my mother might do something violent. Afraid she would cause a scene and embarrass us. Afraid she would get so tired and worn that she'd drift into another lane and kill someone. Afraid she'd harm herself. Afraid she would ask us to care for her.

After twenty years, I began to tell the stories—to siblings, to close friends, to therapists, to myself. Eventually my siblings and I gathered the courage to confront our mother. We told her she was ill. We told her she needed medication and help. We told her she scared us. We told her she was not welcome in our homes unless she took medication. My mother listened. She did not defend or deny or argue against anything we said. She told us she was tired. She told us she needed help.

And then she continued driving.

———

Eighteen months before my father died, he and I spent three days together at a remote Episcopal church and retreat house on the Northern California coast. We had recently had a falling out. Finally in touch with my hurt and anger, I wrote him a screed pointing out his hypocrisies. He wrote me back matching my anger but then offered to fly into town to meet me for dinner to talk things out. I told him not to bother unless he was willing to spend much more time than a dinner. We negotiated schedules and agreed to spend three days together. This would be the most focused time I'd ever had alone with my father.

The church was made of redwood planks, set back in the trees along an inlet on the Pacific coast. The priest gave us a key and then left us on our own. Our rooms were above the sanctuary, with single-pane windows that looked out onto the fog-shrouded water. Between our bedrooms we had a large sitting area with a brick fireplace. We spent the first night by the fire, going back to the beginning. Origins. His childhood. The beginning of his career. His relationship with my mother. My childhood.

We talked long after midnight, slept a handful of hours, and then began again. The divorce. My childhood dreams and hurt. The way he abandoned us to a mentally ill mother. My own spiritual awakenings. Falling in love with my wife. My career struggles and doubts. The way my children were transforming my sense of self. We talked nonstop, listening, asking questions, widening our perspective of one another.

On the second evening, sometime after midnight, I confessed to my father what a burden it was to be told to live a storied life of passion. "What about the ordinary?" I countered. "Isn't loving someone mostly about the ordinary— the day-to-day commitments of making breakfast, doing laundry, tucking children into bed, providing a life that is predictable, safe, and stable? Wasn't this what love looked like? Wasn't most of life common?" When he dismissed the ordinary, he dismissed his children, his home life, his family, me. And did he know what a burden it was to be told that a spiritual life was measured according to passion and excitement, when life was mostly filled with routine?

Dad stopped talking and headed to bed. Early the next morning, before I awoke, he packed his bags and loaded his car. When I came down into the church kitchen, he was waiting for me. He told me he was leaving a day early. Bewildered, I asked why.

"You really hurt me last night."

"How?"

"Do you know how many people thank me for encouraging them to live a passionate life? You know how lucky you are to have a father who wants you to live a passionate life?"

Wearily, I replied, "I am grateful for the encouragement to live a passionate life, Dad. But my life doesn't feel like a Bible story. It's much more muddled and mundane."

I don't know what it was—the emotion with which I spoke, the helplessness in my voice, the raw appeal to be heard—but I remember my dad softening, quieting. We sort of stood around for a while in the kitchen, and then he said, "Okay. Let's start over. Go back to the beginning. I really do want to hear. Tell me about your life."

And so I did. For the rest of the day and on into the night I told what had been hidden inside. And my dad listened. And I became a little more healed, a little more myself.

———

Author and teacher Tristine Rainer says story is "what you wanted, how you struggled, and what you realized out of that struggle." She calls this formula for autobiographical storytelling "following the desireline." As a boy I desired what all children want. I wanted warmth. I wanted to be safe. I wanted to be seen and delighted in. I wanted to be liked (not just loved). How does the struggle get resolved? How do we get free from what we've lived? By being *heard*.

It's no surprise that hiding my childhood stories was ultimately self-damaging. My wife sensed my deep suffering, and many evenings after our children were asleep, she would sit with me asking questions, trying to help me dig down to the source. She asked about my mother. The truth about what was so painful. The moments when I experienced terror or shame. The unspeakable, unmet childhood needs and longings. The guilt. She asked about my father. The anger at his absence. The frustration in failing to attract his attention. The embarrassment and betrayal I felt from his affair.

Sometimes I felt my body freeze in the face of these simple questions. Other times I had to get up and leave the room. She could feel I was trapped but knew there was hope for me to get free. "It's okay to tell me," she said. "What was it like?" Her patience, her love, the safety of her presence allowed my stories to be exorcised. I invited her, and eventually others, inside the catacombs. I described the images I kept secret, unveiled the roots of my shame, my rage, my anger, my guilt. And the story began to shift.

From my father, I learned the power of telling stories. From my mother, I learned the messy complexity of life experience that doesn't fit neatly into a storyline. What I had to learn on my own was that the power of storytelling was not in the telling—it was in the listening.

The transformation occurs in the space between one heart and another. To be heard by someone who is present, open, and caring is to be led into freedom. For several years my wife, close friends, siblings, therapists, and mentors spent long periods of time sitting patiently with me, asking questions, inviting me to contemplate my collected memories, helping me feel and accept and cultivate some tenderness for what I have lived.

4

COMING-OUT PARADE

Philosopher and author Alain de Botton was hired by Heathrow Airport to spend a week as a writer-in-residence. He was given full access to all regions of the airport and asked to reflect and write on what one of the busiest transportation centers in the world reveals about the modern human being. One day, de Botton stationed himself for eight hours outside one of Heathrow's primary arrival halls where family and friends gather to meet their loved ones. As an exercise, de Botton observed the face of each traveler as they exited the airport. He noticed that every person, every single one, took a moment to glance at the faces of waiting people. Even when they knew there would be no one waiting for them—they left their own car at the airport, they reserved a train ticket—still they looked. *Maybe. Maybe my husband is here to surprise me. Maybe one of my grown children decided to meet me. Maybe I know someone. Maybe one of these faces is waiting for me.*

De Botton reflects that in these moments, each human being unknowingly revealed the fundamental hope that waits beneath all our activity: that we might be seen and welcomed.

———

I am looking for people willing to share a story for an upcoming event with the theme "Tales from Childhood." Word gets around, and a young father reaches out to me in an email. "I have a story that needs to be told. I don't want to tell it. But I need to tell it." I know Sean from around town. He is called "Mr. Baseball" for his success as a high school coach and private baseball trainer. I write Sean back and assure him he does not need to tell any story he is not comfortable sharing. He refuses to take the out. "No. I need to do this."

We set a meeting at a church fellowship hall. The stress around his eyes and the tension in his shoulders are palpable. We find a quiet corner, and Sean begins his story. *My earliest memory of my mother is listening to her sing. I would sit on her lap by the radiator, and she would hold me and rock me in a chair and sing to me in Spanish.* His voice catches. His eyes fill with tears. I sit quietly, patiently, and let myself feel the unspoken pain. He pushes forward.

He was raised in New York City, his mother Puerto Rican, his father Irish. It was a large Catholic family. Working class. His father served as a firefighter, and his mother cleaned the local church at night. A memory comes to him:

Sometimes Mom would take all of us kids to the church with her to clean. I loved those nights. We felt so special. Mom would unlock the doors and we would have the whole sanctuary to ourselves. Mom would make a game, tell all of us to run up and down the pews and see how much paper we could collect. Sometimes we would find loose change. It was like a treasure hunt. Then she'd wax the floors, and we'd put rags on our feet and skate up and down the aisles, polishing. We loved it. He smiles at the warmth of the memory.

I didn't realize until my older sister told me years later that Mom cleaned the church because we were poor. She cleaned the church so that we could go to the Catholic school for free. His eyes glance away, and I can sense embarrassment.

I'm in sixth grade, and I notice this boy, this friend of mine, passing out birthday invitations. I had known this kid since I was five. We played on the same baseball team. I had been to every one of his birthday parties since we were little. I see him hand out invitations to most of the other boys in our class, but not to me. So I go up to him and say, "Hey, Nick, where's my birthday invitation?" Nick says, "I don't have one. You're not invited." I don't understand. So I ask him, "Why? Everyone else is invited. Why not me?" And he says, "You're a spic. I don't want any spics at my party."

I had never heard this word. I had no idea what it meant. So I just said, "No, I'm not." By now some of the other boys have gathered around, and Nick starts laughing and says, "Listen, your mother cleans the church, right? She's Puerto Rican. Puerto Ricans clean up garbage. Puerto Ricans are spics."

Sean feels the insult to his mother. The intimacy and fun he felt as the family cleaned the sanctuary is suddenly replaced with shame. Without thinking, he cocks his fist and slams Nick in the face. He is expelled from school for a week. His mother is furious. She walks him home from school in silence. When they get home, she asks why he would do such a stupid thing.

He tells her. He tells her Nick has excluded him from his birthday party. He tells her the racial slur, the insult about being Puerto Rican. *My mother's face changed immediately from anger to fear. She was on the verge of punishing me, but when she heard what had happened, she got quiet and had this really scared look in her eyes. I'll never forget that look. And then she said, "When you go back to school you need to tell Nick and the other boys that you are Spanish. Tell them your mother is from Spain, not Puerto Rico."*

He is shaken by the fear he senses in his mother and is confused by her instructions. Why lie about his identity? Is it dangerous to be Puerto Rican? Not knowing why, he suddenly feels deeply embarrassed of his mother, his family, his identity. A fissure begins inside his heart, separating him from his mother, his family, his heritage, himself.

Six years later, Sean leaves home. When asked about his racial identity he says he's Spanish, but he learns quickly that being Spanish does not protect him from the negative racial stereotypes some people hold toward Hispanics. So in early adulthood, he starts wearing Italian T-shirts. He learns a few Italian phrases and slang words. He knows that his racial appearance is ambiguous because of the blend of Irish and Puerto Rican traits he's inherited. He displays posters of Italy in his room, buys the Godfather trilogy and keeps it on a shelf so everyone can see it. His last name is Gallagher, which is unmistakably Irish, but his skin is dark. So he keeps the Italian paraphernalia visible so that no one will figure out his background.

I never actually told anyone I was Italian. I just made a lot of references to Italy. And when someone would ask me about my ethnic heritage, I would just say an Italian phrase and folks would say, "Okay, so you're Italian," and I wouldn't correct them.

Together we work on his story. He is concerned that parents who have entrusted him with their kids will be upset. He worries people will judge his character and he will lose his coaching position. But it is time. He is determined to claim his true identity. He wants to be seen and received.

The night comes for the community storytelling event and the room is packed. We have some music and then the tellers begin to share their stories. When Sean is introduced he walks forward, then stands silent before the microphone. He is unable to speak. The emotion is too great. Sean is an athlete. He is a confident and commanding coach. But sharing his story with his neighbors and friends is terrifying.

The audience can feel the vulnerability, and they begin to whisper encouragement. "It's okay." "Take your time." "It's all right." "Breathe."

Finally, he begins. He describes the closeness he felt toward his mother. The racial bullying that shattered his sense of self. The overwhelming shame and fear. The effort to distance himself from his mother and his heritage. The lies about his ethnicity. The false identity he assumed with families and students in our town. He ends his story with this: "So I needed to tell this story to you. I need to stop hiding. I need to say to you, and to myself, something I've been terrified to admit ever since that incident in sixth grade: My name is Sean Gallagher. And I am Puerto Rican." He scans the faces of the audience. Immediately, people rise to their feet and applaud.

Social justice facilitator and healer Adrienne Maree Brown reflects on how many Black, Indigenous, and other people of color feel trapped within a world imagined by white people—a world that depicts anyone other than white, heteronormative people as "enemy, fright, other." These stories often have violent, real-world consequences. They also function like restrictive clothing on the self-understanding and self-expression of those they target. Such stories are corsets, hobble skirts, foot bindings, straitjackets. Author Rebecca Solnit suggests, "I think of stories as costumes we try on. Maybe it's important to know that you can take them off, that when you pause your story you're naked and know yourself in another way."

One of the ways people get free is by telling a different story, a story based on the particular truths of what they have lived. It is possible to story our way out from shame, out from family narratives, out from racist and misogynistic worldviews. This is storytelling as liberation. And when someone escapes—when someone cuts the bars, digs the tunnel, leaps over the prison walls, and streaks, butt naked, through the public square—they become a sign of hope, a revelation.

In the mid-1990s, psychologists Marshall Duke and Robyn Fivush were trying to figure out what elements would strengthen families and help children overcome at-risk environments. They discovered that the children who knew stories from their family—origin stories, stories of how parents met and fell in love, stories of family successes and failures—had the best chance of developing a strong sense of self and an inner resiliency. Eventually they developed the "Do You Know?" scale, a list of twenty questions designed to see if a child knew stories from their family. Examples include: Do you know how your parents met? Do you know where your mother grew up? Do you know what went on when you were born? Do you know some of the lessons your parents learned from good and bad experiences? Young people who knew these stories from their families showed higher well-being in a variety of indicators, including self-esteem, academic competence, levels of anxiety, social competence, and general behavior.

It wasn't the accumulation of various historical facts that made children competent and resilient; it was the relationships and interactions in which these stories were communicated that strengthened a child. In other words, knowing family stories meant a child had spent long periods of time listening and talking with parents, grandparents, or other members of their family. The stories were embedded within a child's relationship with their family. Without the relationships, the stories had no power. As Marshall Duke writes, "In order to hear family stories, people need to sit down with one another and not be distracted. Some people have to talk and some have to listen. The stories need to be told over and over and the times of sitting together need to be multiple and occur over many years." Duke and Fivush discovered that most family stories were transferred by mothers and grandmothers, often during family dinners, vacations, and other family gatherings. The stories became a continuation of these relationships and connected a child across generations, helping children foster what Duke and Fivush call the "intergenerational self": a sense that they are part of a community larger than themselves.

There are three kinds of family narratives, according to Duke and Fivush, each with differing impacts on a child's sense of strength and competency. There is the ascending story: tales of success, stories of grandparents moving from rags to riches, of pulling oneself up by the bootstraps. The second type of narrative is primarily tragic, a descending narrative of failure and misfortune: "Once upon a time we were on top of the world, and then we lost everything."

The stories that offer the greatest strength to a child, however, are those stories that oscillate. The family stories that help children develop the intergenerational self are the stories that show resiliency despite varying circumstances: "We've had good times and bad times, but through it all we stuck together."

━━━

A friend told me about a class exercise he experienced as a graduate student. The professor said, "Write down thirty statements that define your identity." My friend wrote down: "I am a man. I am a husband. I am a father. I am African American. I am the descendant of enslaved people. I am a graduate student. I am a friend. I am funny."

The professor then instructed, "Now order them one to thirty, from the identities that are most important down to the ones least important to your sense of self." He did as he was told.

Once everyone had completed the task, the professor said, "Now cross off the last one and as you do, imagine that it is erased." Everyone was silent. The professor continued, "Now cross off the second-to-last one and imagine it is erased." Another moment of silence. The professor continued until all the labels—all the descriptors and identifiers everyone had used to describe themselves—were removed.

I asked my friend what it was like to imagine having no labels. "It was scary without these statements—without the stories I was told, and without the stories I told about myself." The professor invited the students to simply sit in the silence, absent of all identities, returning to the sense of self that existed just before the moment of birth.

He asked the class, "Who are you now?" He let the students quietly meditate on that question for about ten minutes. Then he instructed everyone to slowly rewrite their identifying statements one at a time, from least important to most important, until they had reconstructed their sense of self.

"What was it like in the silence, in the absence of identity?" I asked.

"Well . . . ," he said, searching for the right words. "There was a kind of freedom. A terrifying freedom."

———

Every fall, the Southern Oregon Pride Parade is held in our town. Like most pride parades across the globe, the event is full of color and music to celebrate and promote equality for LGBTQ people. Although there is still much work to be done around the rights of the LGBTQ community, recent years have brought a measure of progress in civil rights and public perceptions. These changes depended on lots of brave storytelling. It took thousands of individuals coming out and sharing their honest experiences, sometimes at great risk, to unlock the hearts and minds of people.

Each year the part of the parade I find most moving is the presence of the families: old and young couples, parents, children, and extended relatives holding hands and walking together, often without a float or fancy car or loud music. It is the most humble part of the parade. My neighbors, colleagues, friends, and acquaintances walk down the street to let others know: This is my family. This is who I am. I am glad to be who I am.

Every once in a while, someone in the parade will see me, and we'll both shout and wave vigorously. In no other setting do I behave this excitedly when encountering my neighbors. Never have I walked into a grocery store, noticed Evelyn standing in the checkout line, and then begun yelling and waving both arms in the air as if she were standing on the deck of the *Queen Mary*, "Evelyn! Yay, Evelyn! Woohoo! Bon voyage!"

But the parade is a community ritual, a public righting of wrongs. It is an invitation for all of us in this town to claim and celebrate our common humanity. So I do my part. I stand on the sidewalk and when Evelyn and her family parade down the street, I try to meet their eyes, I call out and wave wildly until we both feel seen and recognized.

I've often wondered what would happen if our community held a Coming-Out Parade the next day. An invitation would be extended to everyone who feels unseen, hidden, trapped within a demeaning storyline. Like the pride parade, there would be an atmosphere of acceptance and welcome. We'd have music, maybe a band that contains all the uncelebrated instruments—flügelhorn, shofar, saw. Local townsfolk would walk down the street holding signs claiming, without shame, unrecognized aspects of their identity.

I cry often.
I am an artist.

I'm bipolar.

I dance naked—a lot.

I'm a woman who doesn't want children.

I'm afraid to get old.

I'm smart.

I don't exercise.

I'm depressed.

I survived abuse.

I love animals more than people.

I miss my mother.

I'm Puerto Rican.

The rest of the town would line the sidewalks—scanning faces, reading signs, cheering, waving, and, from time to time, running out to welcome those who are trying to get free.

5

PURE MEDICINE

My two sons spent a summer break during college traveling around Ireland. One night they found themselves at the Crane Bar in Galway—a historic pub where they'd been told the best traditional music could be found. It was a slow weekday evening, the room half full with locals. Up front the Galway Ramblers sang and played. At one point the guitarist noticed my sons watching his hands and asked if they were musicians. Two minutes later the boys were playing guitar and mandolin along with the band. The session ended, and when my sons went to leave, the main singer told them the Ramblers would be playing a late-night gig and would expect my sons to perform as the opening act.

Noah and Joseph walked the seaside town, found a meal, and then returned to the Crane for the evening performance. The pub was crowded, but a few band members spotted Noah and Joseph and waved them forward. Pints of Guinness were placed in their hands and, before they could get settled, the lead singer of the Ramblers handed them instruments and introduced them to the room. After a few songs, the boys thanked the audience and went to sit down, but the Ramblers insisted they sit with the band. This was exactly the kind of magical encounter my sons had dreamed of having in Ireland. Long into the night, they sat among the musicians swapping songs, drinking pints, and sharing stories.

Two years later, my son Joseph was studying abroad at Trinity College in Dublin. It had been a bit of a lonely semester. He hadn't connected with the students in his program as he had hoped. On his twentieth birthday, he awoke feeling ill and nauseated. It was his first birthday away from home, away from close friends and family. And now, on top of the loneliness, he was sick. Joseph stayed in bed most of the day, miserable and depressed. Then he thought of Galway, the Crane, and that magical evening over two years earlier. Still feeling under the weather, he packed a backpack and walked downtown to catch the last bus to Galway. Arriving around ten at night, still unwell, with two hours officially left on his birthday, he shouldered his backpack and made his way to the Crane. It was a cold November evening. The sidewalks were empty, but he heard music as he approached the historic pub.

Joseph opened the door, stepped inside, and looked around. Immediately the band stopped playing, and the guitarist called out, "Joseph! Where's your brother? Get up here and give us a song." Those in the pub turned and watched as Joseph, slightly embarrassed, made his way to the front. Someone got him a chair, a mandolin was placed in his hand, and a pint of Guinness set before him. For the next three hours Joseph played and sang along with the Ramblers. "It was like medicine," he told us later. And the illness? "It just went away."

There are certain "pure medicines" that every wisdom tradition makes available to the lost and disheartened. Silence. Song. Story. These are the ancient remedies to nourish the withered soul. These are the practices that cause the sap to rise. These are the sacred pathways that bring us health, a sense of peace, a sense of home. These are the storehouses that hold the treasured values of a culture and remind us that we belong to one another.

There has never been a time in history when humans consumed as many stories as we do today. If stories are relational, if their power is to connect us to others, to our own hearts, our values, and the natural world, then why are we so estranged from one another? Why is the earth suffering from such mindless exploitation? Why are there skyrocketing increases in depression? Why has the United Kingdom recently decided to appoint a minister of loneliness?

Our culture is awash with stories—the vast majority of which contain no medicinal properties. We spend our days and nights gorging on stories, our eyes filled with streaming television shows, our ears crowded with podcasts, our minds flung left and right from online news. We stare at screens, flooding our bodies with stories that distort our longings. Stories that sow fear and malice. Stories that divide and diminish. Stories that label one group "good guys" and the other "not fully human." We stay up late, scanning through videos that make us sick with anxiety and self-judgment. We sit side by side, alone in the light of our phones, consuming stories built for branding. We listen to stories that titillate. Stories that overwhelm our pleasure centers. Stories that fill our minds with gnawing envy. Stories that redirect our deepest yearnings. Stories that reduce us to our hungers. Stories that leave us lonely and wanting. And when we finally turn off the screens—tired, defeated—we fall asleep empty and restless, not knowing why.

Over half a million marketers within the United States call themselves "storytellers," according to a recent analysis of online profiles. What is the hope of these storytellers? What stories are they trying to tell? Attracting, keeping, and manipulating our attention seems to be the primary aim. Streaming television, social media "stories," internet videos aimed at every demographic are offered to us each day as emotional stimulants, escape mechanisms to divert us from the mundane, the demeaning, the frightful. The voracious and continual consumption of stories can render all stories, even the most sacred, meaningless.

If we don't pay attention to the relational nature of stories—both in their telling and in what is told—then we end up with stories (no matter how powerful their content) that function as junk food for the soul. Or worse, instruments of control and sedation. It is clear we have little self-control over our storytelling devices. We spend more than eleven hours a day consuming media. Adam Alter, author of *Irresistible*, cites a survey in which young adults were asked if they would prefer a broken bone or a broken phone. Forty-six percent chose the broken bone. Alter relates, "When you watch them make the decision . . . even those who say they'd rather have a broken phone, agonize."

Unchecked, pursued mindlessly without limits, our distractions will ruin us. But what is it that these desires ultimately seek? Life is hard. Loss is real. Suffering comes to each of us. Is it so wrong to seek a little distraction, a respite from the heaviness, the monotony, the overwhelming speed and activity of our world?

The wish to be lost in a story is a basic human desire. As neuroscientists are discovering, we have story-loving brains that are drawn toward the vicarious tensions, discoveries, and release that stories provide. The attraction toward story is not simply for the hit of dopamine; ultimately what propels us to "binge" on story after story is the yearning to connect. The yearning to feel our deeper capacities for the pain and pleasure of living. The yearning for relationship. The yearning to share in the lives of others. The yearning for a respite from the anxious struggles of our own lives. These are natural human desires that are unfortunately exploited by the media and various political and corporate interests. This misdirection and overindulgence of our basic human longings for life and connection harms us. We sleep less. We play less. We think less. We neglect our relationships.

Passively giving our story-loving attention to streaming television and social media weakens our imagination, cultivates false impressions of the world, and distracts us from the depth and purpose our souls seek. Sadly, recent studies reveal that the more we consume television and social media, the less alive we become. The more stories we imbibe, the more we feel disconnected, depressed, and unsatisfied.

And we know this.

We know we are spending too much time in front of screens. We know we need to disconnect. We know we are giving too much of our life's energy to entertainment. We know we need more time outdoors. We know our relationships are suffering. We know our bodies are sleep deprived. We know our hearts and minds are overstimulated and overwhelmed. We know this is not the life we long to live. But what do we do?

In 2012, my father-in-law, a retired teacher, took our family on a trip to Europe. He wanted his grandkids to experience the history, cities, and artwork of Europe. We carefully crafted our three-week itinerary: London, Paris, Venice, Amsterdam, Rome, and other historic destinations. Halfway into the trip we were in Florence, Italy, to see some of the great architecture and works of art from the Italian Renaissance. Tourists from around the world crowded the streets. The line to the Accademia Gallery, which houses Michelangelo's statue of *David*, wrapped around the block.

As we finally entered the gallery and shuffled our way toward the towering sculpture, a young man in track shorts and tank top squeezed by me and ran zigzag through the gaps in the crowd, past the statue of *David*, and out toward the exit. A few minutes later a young woman, sporting a similar uniform, pushed by us and ran through the crowd, past the statue, and out the exit. Every few minutes a runner would weave his or her way through the people, running past all the classic works of art. A bit irritated, I assumed some track team was visiting Florence and decided to use the museum for their workout.

When we exited the gallery, I asked one of the employees about the runners. He told me it was actually a piece of performance art created by a local Italian artist to reflect the harried tourists who anxiously speed through the celebrated museums seeking to consume as many works of art as possible but end up leaving untouched and unchanged by the beauty, the truth, the transcendence that each carefully crafted work sought to evoke.

The runners in the Accademia had an impact on my family. We found ourselves discussing how much art our minds and hearts could reasonably absorb, and how much time it really takes to perceive and feel the intention of the artist. We began leaving museums after just an hour or two, once we noticed our brains were satiated.

Not long after our time in Florence, we were in Paris, walking the mile-and-a-half length of the most famous avenue in the world, the Champs-Élysées. We began at the Louvre, walked through the Palace Gardens, and then made our way along the wide sidewalks and manicured trees toward the iconic Arc de Triomphe. The avenue was crowded with people rushing in and out of shops and cafés. At one point, someone in our family noticed we were moving at the pace of the bustling crowd. We remembered the Italian runners in the Accademia, and suddenly an idea emerged. What if instead of hurrying past the palaces, gardens, theaters, and historic sites along the Champs-Élysées, we intentionally walked as slowly as possible? My wife and I, our three children, our two nieces, and my wife's brother all slowed our walking to glacial speed. Like a group of meditative monks, we crept contemplatively down the sidewalk. People began to stop and watch. Crowds parted in front of us. Some, mostly children, joined the snail-like procession. For thirty minutes we continued in a slow, meditative stroll while others sped by.

That was ten years ago. Yet our children still talk about that experience—vividly recalling the breeze, the sun, the light on the buildings, the stillness, and the presence they felt amid the wondrous architecture and landscapes of the great avenue. In contrast, a number of other excursions from that summer in Europe remain either blurred or semi-forgotten. Our bodies were too overworked, our senses too wearied to fully appreciate all the sights and sounds. Not true of that afternoon in Paris. Slow-walking the Champs-Élysées, we moved at the speed of living and received the beauty around us.

Part of the suffering of this present age is the inability to discern what brings life and what brings death. The voracious, mindless consumption of stories leaves us forgetting what makes us human. We remain ignorant of their potential to heal or inflict damage, numb or awaken us to the life we are longing to embody. In the modern world we hunger not only for nutrient-rich stories, full of meaning and connection, but also for face-to-face gatherings, enlivening relationships, places of deep presence where the story, the teller, and those listening can find the connections they seek. In a digital world, we long for analog.

Who would we be if instead of three hours a day on our phones or in front of screens, we spent three hours a day in nature? Three hours a day reading books? Three hours a day working in the garden? Three hours a day with our families? Three hours a day serving our communities? Who would we be today if for the past year we had devoted three hours a day to simply feeling the life within and around us?

For several years, every Tuesday night my wife, daughter, and I would get together with two other couples for dinner. Each couple took turns hosting, so the meal moved from home to home. Sometimes our various young adult children joined us when they were in town. At some point during the meal, someone would tell a story that inevitably prompted a memory from someone else. And then we were off—each person sharing their own recollection on the topic—first kiss, a time we got in trouble, a teacher who changed our life, a lost love, an injustice we suffered. Eventually it would get late. The stories would wane. The table would be cleared. We'd gather coats and hats, hug, and say our goodbyes. Each family would return home with hearts warmed, spirits calmed, and souls renewed.

Storytelling is being human together. We tell stories to savor the pleasures of living. We share stories to help one another remember who we are and what matters. We tell stories to weave our lives together. We tell stories to keep our souls intact when suffering overtakes us. This is story as medicine. This is how story can save us.

INTERLUDE

CLARA

He was tall and walked like a man who had spent a year at sea. He wore large hearing aids and spoke with rounded consonants. There was something elegant, almost regal about the way he carried himself. His listening was focused and well-mannered. He dressed in western garb, silver bolo ties, and pearl-snap shirts. He was well-read, with what he called a "photographic memory" that enabled him to quote whole poems and long passages from books he'd read decades earlier. He was a poet, a Jungian therapist, a former professor at Notre Dame, an Episcopal priest, and author of more than forty books on the spiritual life. And he was my teacher, my friend, my spiritual mentor. His name was Morton Kelsey. I met him when I was twenty-six and he was seventy-five. He was leading a contemplative retreat at a Franciscan convent in Portland, Oregon. I was a young man in the middle of an identity crisis.

Morton helped me find my way through that crisis. He introduced me to silence, prayer, and meditation. He listened to me. Cared for me. And he taught me a way of seeing myself and the world that formed me personally and professionally. After that retreat we began a correspondence and friendship. Morton frequently traveled to San Francisco to lead retreats at the seminary I was attending. When he did, I provided transportation, hosted him in the seminary guesthouse, and shared meals with him. On a number of occasions, I assisted him while he led retreats. No matter the subject, Morton liked to start a retreat by placing participants in small groups and inviting each person to share their life story. To model this process, he would tell his own life story. I heard him share his story many times. It was heartbreaking.

He was born a "blue baby" in rural Illinois in 1917. Five weeks premature, Morton's skin was thin and transparent, his head disproportionately large, his fingernails and toenails not yet fully formed. When he was older and asked his parents about a ridge on the back of his head, they told him it was caused by forceps that crushed his head at birth.

In old letters Morton discovered that when his mother first saw him she rejected him, called him "hideous." She had even written a letter to her sister to tell her she had "given birth to a monster." Certain that this tiny, premature baby would soon die, she refused to care for him. She had to be forced by her husband and doctor to nurse him. In sharing his story Morton would relate, "According to letters from my father, I was rarely held. I was so tiny, my parents kept me in a shoe box placed next to a woodstove for warmth. My father wrote that he often expected to find me dead in the morning. But for whatever reason, I lived."

When Morton was six months old, his family moved to Palmerton, Pennsylvania, a company town built to house employees for the new zinc-smelting plant. Morton's father was hired as the company manager. Morton's mother had duties as the wife of the company manager and was eager to spend time away from her infant. Day after day she was forced to nurse Morton, but otherwise she rarely held him.

As a baby, Morton was diagnosed with mild cerebral palsy and drooled constantly. He also suffered from hearing loss, and only after a routine check-up in college was it discovered that he was nearly deaf. To adapt, he learned to read lips as a child. But all through his growing-up years, his speech was slurred. His parents believed their youngest son, with cerebral palsy and undiagnosed hearing loss, was unfit for the world and would need to live an institutionalized life.

"My parents gave me just enough love to keep me alive," Morton often quipped. As soon as he was weaned, Morton was placed in a detached cottage apart from the main house. A fourteen-year-old girl from town was hired to live in the cottage and provide full-time care for Morton. For his first four years he lived a life separate from his brother, mother, and father.

When he was four, a local doctor recommended that Morton be placed in a home for disabled children. As part of the intake he was given a Stanford-Binet intelligence test. His scores were so high that the local school officials had Morton take the test a second time. Again, his intelligence scores were near the top of the scale. Following this test, Morton was brought home and for the first time received love and acceptance from his parents as a full son. Years of rejection, however, had already inflicted deep damage on his soul and psyche.

You can imagine what that kind of early neglect does to a person. Predictably, Morton suffered from extreme bouts of depression and anxiety as an adolescent and young adult. Although he was bright and received high grades and scholarships to college, he struggled constantly with thoughts of hurting himself. In his early twenties, filled with feelings of worthlessness and self-hatred, he decided to end his life. One afternoon he took his father's rifle and walked up into the Allegheny Mountains, fully prepared to die by suicide. He waited until night descended, headed out to a large rock formation, lay on his back looking up at the stars, and waited for midnight.

And then.

Just as he prepared to leave his life, a song came to him. *It was not a song heard through the ears. It was deeper than that. It was a song that came from the rocks and trees and stars and earth. It entered my body from all directions. It was a sort of lullaby. A song of love and comfort and warmth.*

This is the turning point in his story. The song Morton hears that night reorders his sense of self. He is disoriented, confused, and buoyed by what he has felt. He wonders if this was some kind of encounter with God, but he has little religious understanding. The next day, still shimmering from his revelation in the mountains, he walks into town and enters the first church he finds. The small-town priest in the neighborhood Episcopal church listens to Morton's story and then invites him to dinner with his family. Over the next year, through the care of the priest, a compassionate therapist, and a variety of spiritual practices, Morton finds a way through the deep rejection and pain of his early childhood. He goes on to graduate school and then seminary. He becomes a husband, a father, a writer, a professor, and a spiritual teacher. This was his story, a story I had heard many times.

In 1994, I picked Morton up from the San Francisco Airport. When we stopped for lunch he said to me, "Something extraordinary has happened." I listened as Morton told me about a recent letter he had received from a woman named Clara. In the letter, the woman said she had come across one of his books and wondered if Morton had ever lived in Palmerton, Pennsylvania. Morton had published many books and was used to receiving letters from readers. He responded to the woman's letter and told her that yes, he had been raised in Palmerton. He then sent her a copy of one of his books, a book of legends from the Seneca tribe that he had been told as a child.

Within days Morton received a reply. Clara wrote back to tell him that she was very familiar with the Seneca tales. In fact, she was the one who told them to Morton when he was a little boy. Clara went on to write:

When I was fourteen years old, your parents hired me to take care of you. You were just an infant, but they placed you in my care, and together we lived in a detached cottage. I felt like I was the luckiest girl in town. Your parents provided a crib for you to sleep in, but unbeknownst to them, you never slept in that crib. You always slept next to me. Your parents rarely held you, but I loved to hold you constantly. As you got older I sang to you and told you stories. For four years you were the center of my life. You were my best friend.

Later she wrote: *I have been looking for you my whole life, Morton. Please come and see me.* Sitting in the restaurant in San Francisco, Morton told me that he had called Clara. He discovered she was ninety-one years old, a retired librarian, still bright and capable, still living in Pennsylvania. She'd never married, never had children of her own. "When I spoke with her, it was as if I'd always known her," he said.

"What are you going to do?" I asked.

"I'm going to go see her."

The next week Morton and his wife flew out to eastern Pennsylvania to visit Clara in her home. She had pictures, seventy-five-year-old snapshots of herself holding Morton as a baby and toddler. Morton had few memories from his early years and almost no photographs. Clara not only had photographs, but even at ninety-one, she remembered the vivid details of Morton's earliest years—what he ate, the toys he enjoyed, the books he liked to look at, his favorite hat. Morton's wife, Barbara, later told me, "They loved each other immediately. It was like a long-lost son returning to his mother."

Throughout the day and into the evening, Morton and Clara sat together side by side. "The image I'll never forget," Barbara told me, "is when we went to leave. We stood in the doorway exchanging goodbyes when Clara leaned forward and hugged Morton. She placed her head on his chest and began to sing. It was a lullaby. It was a song she had sung to Morton when he was a baby." Suddenly Morton began to weep. "She sang, and he wept these deep tears. I had no idea why he was so moved."

The song ended, and they said their goodbyes. Morton was silent for a long time. Finally he spoke to his wife. "Do you know the song Clara sang? The lullaby she sang to me as a child? That was the same song that came to me in the mountains all those years ago when I was planning to end my life."

Suddenly, in his late seventies, Morton had to change his life story. No longer was his the story about a child who was rejected and unloved. He now talked about Clara, his surrogate mother, who loved and cared for him during the years of separation from his parents. No longer was the story of his early life one of constant isolation. It was now the story of being cared for by a loving fourteen-year-old girl despite his parents' neglect. It was now the story of a caregiver who saw Morton's beauty despite his ailments, a girl who was unwilling to share his parents' belief that he was a damaged and hopeless child. Morton said that after meeting Clara, something inside him knew that he had been deeply loved.

The last time I visited Morton in his home in San Diego, he showed me a picture of Clara taken at her high school graduation, the year she moved away from Palmerton. After Clara sent it to him, Morton had the picture enlarged and framed. He kept it by his bed during the last seven years of his life. "This beautiful, kindly young woman is my image of love," he later wrote. "Its patience, its invincible, healing power."

Many of us live our lives with few recollections of the people who truly saw us and loved us—teachers who said kind words, nurses who cared for us, extended family who looked at us with delight. And yet these moments of grace and love are like mountain springs from which water can still be drawn. Somehow, deep within us, these encounters with love are still present in our bodies, waiting within our unconscious memories. We hear echoes of these experiences in our longings for love, for home, for acceptance.

Maybe all of us have a Clara, a soul who sits somewhere unbeknownst, recalling us with delight. Someone who looked at us and cared for us, who let us know that we had value and worth. Someone who became for us, at least in one moment, the face of love.

6

THE HEARTH

A few years ago I came across an article by an American writer and wine connoisseur who considered himself an expert in the science and study of wine. The article was about an experience he had while researching winemaking across Italy. At a stop in Tuscany he met with one of the premier traditional winemakers. For generations this man's family had grown and harvested grapes on the same land. While interviewing this elderly Italian vintner, the writer mentioned the popular one to a hundred point system developed by Robert Parker to rate the quality of wines. The elderly man shook his head and said, "Impossible to do. Wine is not a number." The American began to defend the idea of the number system, the way wine could be broken down into particulars and measured according to certain qualities. The winemaker listened but did not respond. When the interview ended, the elderly man invited the writer back to his vineyard for lunch the next afternoon.

The following day the young writer was led into the heart of the vineyard where workers and family members were preparing for a late afternoon meal. Tables were lined up between rows of autumn grapevines with leaves the color of fire. People carried baskets of food from the main house. Young children placed flowers on the table. Cloth napkins, glasses, wooden bowls, and small ceramic plates were set out.

The meal was simple. Bread, cheeses, cured meats, olives, garden vegetables. An enormous black cauldron filled with white bean, sausage, and fennel root soup was placed over an open fire. Glasses were filled with water pumped from a nearby well. Clay pitchers with red wine were set within arms' reach.

For several hours there was conversation, laughter, and storytelling around the table. The kids played soccer between the rows of grapes. The light in the vineyard was exquisite; the food was full of homegrown flavors. And the wine? The wine was excellent, the best he'd tasted in months of travel.

As the meal came to a close, the American was certain the old vintner had invited him to the meal to show off one of his premier wines. He asked his host to identify the wine. "First," the old man said with a twinkle in his eye, "tell me the number you would give it according to the rating system." Without hesitation the writer said, "Somewhere in the mid-nineties. Ninety-four, ninety-five."

The old man smiled. "What we drank was a simple table wine. Nothing special. It was given a rating of seventy-eight."

The young writer was dumbfounded. How could that be? He had a trained palate. He was well versed in identifying the specific qualities and nuances for rating wines. How could his senses be so off? The old Italian noticed the young man's confusion and explained. Wine is about relationship. The place, the people, the occasion, the light in the room, the state of your own heart when you drink it. Wine brings out and heightens the relationships around the meal. When you isolate wine as a product—ignoring the context, dissecting, measuring, and rating the various parts—it loses its power. It loses its soul. At that point, you are no longer drinking wine. You are simply stimulating your tongue.

In 2009, the church I attended began a meal and shower service for the area's homeless population. I noticed the volunteers who led this endeavor made a concerted effort to meet the physical needs of local families and individuals without expecting any participation in the church. The new program was simply a way of serving people on the margins.

While volunteering in this project, it occurred to me that while some populations in our town suffered from physical poverty, at least as many suffered from loneliness and a kind of spiritual poverty: loss of relationship to self, others, the earth, the Sacred. I wondered if there was a way to address the relational and spiritual needs of people without asking them to adhere to any particular belief system. Could a nonreligious, spiritual "shelter" be created that matched our homeless shelter?

In every good story something dies so that something new can be born. My story was that I had spent most of my adult life working within Christian institutions. I had been formed in the practices of Christian community. I knew these skills were needed outside of the church and wondered if there was a way to step outside of a religious context and use my gifts to serve the larger public.

One day as I was grappling with these questions, a friend of mine suggested I look into the Moth in New York City. The Moth is a storytelling series in which people are invited to share a personal story in front of a live audience. I recognized the power of this model, but I wanted to find a way to engage story not as entertainment but as a community practice for cultivating compassion.

In an interview, author Barry Lopez relates how a traditional Native American storyteller taught him the distinction between authentic and inauthentic stories. "An authentic story is about us, an inauthentic story is about you." I wanted to create a space for authentic stories that would function as a source of connection. To help make this happen, I borrowed practices from spiritual communities—silence, song, meaning-making, shared food and drink, an offering of funds to give to a local charity, a moral imperative to serve the greater good.

I decided to hold the first community storytelling event on Valentine's Day. I went to the hardware store, barbershop, school gatherings, and sporting events around town, asking people if they might be willing to share a love story from their own lives to raise money for the local food bank. Within a couple of months, I had six locals willing to tell a story. I made posters, set up a quick website, put ads in the local newspapers, and decided on a five-dollar door charge to benefit the food bank. I booked a pub and recruited some musician friends. I named this new storytelling gathering The Hearth. The motto was "Real Stories by Regular Folks."

I invited the six tellers to my home to practice. The stories they wanted to share were unexpected. None of them had a traditional romantic love story. Instead, they brought stories of divorce, family tensions, and struggles to quiet inner voices of self-hatred. I was surprised. What drove these people to want to share such intimate experiences? Late into the night, this group of strangers sat in my front room helping each other craft their stories, responding to one another with encouragement and support. Once the last teller felt confident in their tale, we all stood and took a collective deep breath. One woman said, "Three hours ago you were all just names to me. Now you feel like family."

Before you do something well, you have to do it badly. Enter the first Hearth gathering. The speaker system sounded like a child's radio. People wanted drinks, but there was only one waitress, and she was in a bad mood. The pub

was overcrowded, causing the manager to send people outside because of fire code. Eventually, he became so nervous
about breaking the law that he just went home.

It was a cold February night in Oregon, but the people
outside wouldn't leave. Instead they propped open doors
and windows so they could hear. This made the room freez-
ing, which caused the people indoors to occasionally shout,
"Close the damn door!"

At the center of the room was a group of bikers—
cyclists, actually—who had been drinking for a couple hours
and were irritated by the crowd. When I stepped up to the
microphone to welcome the audience, these cyclists began
to heckle, "Shut the hell up!" They were blunt, lacked cleverness. We had invaded their bar, and they were irritated.
I stood and spoke my introductions into the muted microphone. "Welcome to The Hearth. Tonight we present real
stories by regular folks. Six brave souls, six local community
members have volunteered to tell a true love story, told in
first person, in ten minutes, without notes . . ."

"Fuck you!" A lanky cyclist in his midseventies shook
his middle finger at me. His buddies cheered. I continued
talking about the local food bank, the evening's beneficiary.
My mouth was praising the food bank, but my mind was
working on a solution to the hecklers. How could I quiet
these drunken men in neon spandex? How could I possibly
win them over?

I began shouting into the microphone. "This is Valentine's Day! A day we celebrate that most elusive and

sought-after human experience! Each one of us hopes to find some human heart, some caring soul, some warm body so overwhelmed with attraction that they're willing to fondle our genitalia!"

I paused. The bicyclists in their short-billed hats were thrown for a moment and then erupted in cheers. *Sheep without a shepherd*, my grandfather always said. *Sheep without a shepherd*. Mr. Middle Finger gave me the thumbs up as if to say, "You're all right, man. You are all right."

The room quieted after the cheers. The men turned their heads and gave me a chance. People leaned forward to hear.

"So the theme tonight is love," I continued. "Every one of us, every beating heart, comes into the world seeking some kind of warmth and acceptance. Some kind of embrace. Some kind of reconciliation. Is there anything we suffer more than the lack of love? Love is the greatest pleasure, love is the deepest pain. Tonight, six neighbors will help us explore this most treasured of all human experiences."

A local musician came forward and played. We passed a bucket to collect money for the food bank. The tellers were then brought up one by one to share their love stories. These were ordinary people, and the experiences they shared were authentic, sometimes humorous, and quite touching. A retired man told about reconciling with his mother-in-law after forty years of resentment. A middle-aged mother talked about the difficulty of dating following a painful divorce. A grade-school teacher shared the struggle to love herself after embodying messages of shame from her parents.

Amid the crackle of the kitchen fryer, the clink and scrape of people eating, and customers' calls for drinks, the storytellers spoke their particular truths into the microphone— their stories more confession than performance. Each person stood and humbly offered a piece of their life, and within the vulnerability of each story, we recognized our own struggle for love.

The third storyteller that evening was a young woman who worked at a local hotel. She had been born and raised in our town and was known by many in the room. Her Valentine's Day story was unusual. At seventeen she had gotten pregnant. Her parents, her friends, and her boyfriend all encouraged her to terminate the pregnancy. She was young, still finishing high school, and in no position to raise a child. But Ellen wanted to have the baby despite the disruption to her life and the tension it caused her family. Alone in her conviction, she faced the shaming remarks from her classmates as her belly grew. Finally the due date came, and her son was born. With her mother and sister at her side, Ellen received her beautiful, healthy baby boy when he was placed on her chest.

"And I felt nothing," she confessed. "It was as if some stranger had handed me their baby. There were no maternal feelings, there was no sense of love or connection. But because I had fought so hard to have this child, I had to keep my feelings secret. I had to pretend everything was wonderful."

Ellen paused and the room went silent.

"For months I felt as if I were a caregiver for someone else's child. I fed him and changed his diapers. I held him when he cried, but I still felt very little warmth. Eventually I got a job at a local hotel. My mother watched the baby while I worked a night shift with a woman who had emigrated from India. After cleaning, paperwork, and doing other tasks the two of us would take a break together."

One night Ellen's coworker shared the story of her courtship and marriage. She explained that in her culture marriages are arranged by parents. She told Ellen that she met her husband only a week before the wedding. In those first months of her marriage she felt estranged, awkward, and depressed. She finally decided she needed to find a way to fall in love with this man. She began to watch and study her partner, looking for his attractive qualities. Little by little, she discovered her new husband's kindness, goodness, and charm—and convinced her heart to fall in love.

Ellen could see her own situation through the story of her workmate. She was in an arranged parenting relationship. She needed to be open and attentive to discover her son's beauty. With a new sense of curiosity and wonder, she began to spend long periods of time gazing at her son. "Over time I started to see how incredibly beautiful he was," she told us. "His dark eyes. His little mouth. I could feel his personality. His sweetness. The way he nestled his face against my neck. The way he smiled. And then it happened. One morning, while looking into his eyes, my heart opened up and I fell madly, deeply in love. Now, five years later, if you were to ask me, 'Who is the great love of your life?' It is my son. And I am so grateful I fought to be his mother."

She paused, then stood back from the microphone. The room broke into applause and we took a break for intermission. Then something unexpected happened. Women from all across the room, even from outside the pub doors, began to make their way to Ellen. Soon five or six women, maybe more, encircled her, confessing their own experiences of estrangement, shame, and inner conflict. Ellen's story had helped free their secrets, and through offering her story, these women found comfort in one another.

———

In many faith traditions, there is no individual salvation. We either all get there or none of us do. There is no individual enlightenment—only enlightenment on behalf of the whole. This is not an American way of thinking. But I believe it is how we actually find our way home—by journeying together.

At this moment in history, it is possible to feed every human being. It is possible to house every human being. It is possible to heal the suffering of every neglected child. It is possible to create a just society. It is possible to heal the environment. To do these things, we have to overcome what philosopher Charles Eisenstein calls the most damaging story in the world: "We are separate."

In this age of increased polarization, division, and social isolation, we are desperate for community. And community, real community, relies on an old technology called, "You had to be there." We have to actually be in the same (real or, depending on the circumstances, virtual) room. We have to listen. We have to tell the truth. We have to practice being together. "Listening is an act of community," Ursula K. Le Guin once wrote. If we create the time and space needed to listen, we soon find the delusions of us and them, friend and enemy, holy and profane dissipate, and we enter into the mysterious, particular truth of you, of me, of us. Gathering to share stories is how we learn to trust one another. It is an exchange of gifts. You talk, I listen. Now I talk, you listen. It's a humble exchange. Image by image, experience by experience, our lives become nourishment to one another. Through listening and speaking we dismantle the barricades.

I saw an interview with the Dalai Lama in which he was read a list of the wars, divisions, and conflicts of the world. "How do we bring people together?" the interviewer asked. His answer? "More picnics." You come together. You share food. You kick a ball around. You sit and talk with your neighbors, sharing food and story and life. Peace by picnic.

———

Like all human beings I want to be changed, transformed— made more whole, more loving, more free. I want to live with a sense of meaningful purpose. I want to coax forth the angel of my better nature. But like all human beings I can't make this happen by force of will (although I keep trying). I need help. I need others. I need friends, companions, wise teachers who know the struggle and who can be trusted to remind me what I'm doing here. I need others to turn the mediocre wine I have made of my life into a source of redemption, wisdom, friendship, and hope.

For over ten years now, The Hearth has invited the local community together to share stories to serve a larger purpose. Each gathering attracts about four hundred people in our small town. Hours before a Hearth event, volunteers come to set up chairs and tables. Local musicians who have prepared songs arrive to tune instruments and do sound checks. Folks arrive with home-baked goods. A local winery drops off donated wine. Other volunteers show up to work the front door and concessions. The designated nonprofit and beneficiary of the evening sets up a table of information about its work—protecting the Klamath River, feeding the homeless, tutoring underprivileged children, teaching anti-racism in the schools, supporting victims of sexual assault. By 6:30 p.m., people are lined up outside ready to pitch in five to fifteen dollars at the door to benefit the featured organization. When the clock turns seven, I take the floor and remind people why we've gathered.

"The Hearth is an evening when we practice community," I say. "Some of us practice by setting up chairs. Some by baking goods. Some by sharing stories. Some by performing music. Some by giving money to the local nonprofit. This is not a performance. We are not here to watch a show. We are here to explore what it means to be human. We are here to listen for ways we are being asked to grow, to act, to serve. We are here because we need one another."

Throughout the evening live music is played. Six community members each come forward and share the truth they have lived—a funny truth, a heroic truth, a tragic truth. Storyteller Elizabeth Ellis refers to storytelling in community as "blowing on the embers of a fire." Every time the people of my town gather to share stories, we are warmed, renewed, home.

7

STORYCATCHER

Leo Tolstoy once said that all great literature could be reduced to two stories: a man goes on a journey, and a stranger comes to town.

I have spent much of my work life as a traveling stranger. The gift I offer as the stranger is that I do not know individuals' stories. And the gift I offer as the traveler is that I will leave. These attributes often make me a safe person to hear confession, a safe person to receive the intimate burdens of others.

When I travel to a town, I find there is the public work and the private work. The public work is the teaching, storytelling, and community facilitation I have been hired to do. The private work is what happens the rest of the time. The hushed conversations in hallways. The written notes placed on the podium. The hurting young man who waits to talk with me after the auditorium has emptied. The haggard father who asks to buy me a beer. This secret, private work is often the most important role I play when I travel to a town. And wherever I am, there are stories yearning to be heard.

There is the young woman whose brother died in childhood. The man whose wife is sleeping with his best friend. The grandmother afraid of dying. The pastor who lost God twenty years ago. The college student who was sexually abused. The therapist who is afraid of her own anger. The motherless daughter. The hospital nurse who hates himself. The environmental activist who pushes tacks into her thighs. The Latinx teacher who felt her ancestors in a dream last night. The father whose son died by suicide. The professor who yearns to know her birth father.

And when I listen—when I truly listen to these honest and broken and beautiful and vulnerable people—what I hear is the sound of longing. What I hear is the human heart crying for release. Release, freedom, peace, something (anything) besides these false impersonations of ourselves. And when I listen, I hear them say: Tell me I matter. Ask me a good question. Echo back to me what I know. Trust me until I trust myself. Remind me why I love my life. Give me a chance to say I'm sorry. Invite me to light a candle for those I love. Help me celebrate what is good in the world and in me. Ask me to tell you my story.

———

When we first meet, she is recovering from an illness. She seems tired, worn down. Her eyes are wary, anxious. What has she gotten herself into? We are in North Wales, near the foothills of Snowdonia, sitting in the upper room of a church fellowship hall. The United Kingdom has just voted to leave the European Union. Many analysts believe that what has been nicknamed Brexit is a sign of growing animosity in the United Kingdom toward immigrants and refugees.

Maitea, with her short black hair and large brown eyes, is Colombian. Married to a Welsh man, she has lived in the north of Wales for most of her adult life. She meets with me because she has a story to tell but doesn't know how to tell it. "I'm not sure what to say, where to begin."

"Just start," I say. "Just tell me what you have."

She talks in ideas. Her desire to help the refugees. Her frustration with the Brexit vote and how it will hurt immigrants. The outpouring of help she has received since starting a charity to assist the refugees. The many differences between Welsh and Colombian culture, especially when it comes to the extended family. "When you have a baby in Colombia, that baby belongs to everyone in the family—grandparents, uncles, aunts, everyone. They are just as responsible for that child as the parents are. When a baby is born, family members come to your home at all hours to hold your baby and make food and care for the child. Sometimes they stay for days or weeks, just being with you and helping take care of the family. Here it is different. I remember when my sister-in-law had a child I immediately made food and went to their home. I didn't make an appointment. The husband answered the door and told me they weren't ready for guests and asked if I could come another time. That does not happen in Colombia. You don't get cleaned up for family. You *are* family."

I have helped many people craft and share stories. Tragedies, comedies, heroic tales, stories of rebirth and resurrection, romances of every shape—girl meets boy, boy meets boy, girl meets cat. People seeking to tell their story to support a cause, eradicate shame, bear witness to an injustice, inspire action, pass on their wisdom to loved ones, express the hilarity of the human condition. And to do this, to put their lives into story, people need an accompanier, a companion, someone who can listen their lives into meaning.

Three years ago Maitea founded a charity to gather food, clothing, and supplies for refugees. Particularly in the wake of the Brexit vote, the charity has attracted a lot of attention. She works many hours each week trying to meet the needs of displaced people while raising her two small children. She has a story she needs to tell, but she is too close to it. It's difficult to find it, to feel it, to put it into words. Together we listen for the thread.

"Tell me about the moment when you decided to help the refugees."

"I was exercising on one of those elliptical machines, looking through my phone, when all of a sudden there was that image of a small boy, a toddler, drowned. It showed up on the news site I read, then on my social media. Everyone was posting it. This little body lying washed up on a beach on some Greek island. I stopped everything. I pulled up the article and read that this boy was part of a family fleeing their country. I just fell to pieces when I saw that picture and read about this poor family—this boy, his siblings, his mother, all drowned. How could this happen? How could we allow this to happen? All they were doing was seeking safety. This was wrong. Someone needed to do something. I had to do something."

We are quiet for a moment. There is emotion in her voice, tears welling up in her eyes.

A question comes to me. "The picture of the boy was in the news all around the world. Millions of people saw that photo, felt badly, but then went about their day. Why did you decide to act when so many others didn't?"

Something flashes across her eyes. Is it anger? Pain? Conviction? She looks at me directly, "Because I know what it's like to lose a son."

This is the story. This is why Maitea is here. This is the story she has lived to tell.

What motivates a person to share their story? Why not stay quiet? There are many reasons. To speak the unspoken truth. To feel the grace of one's own life. To extract sorrow. To hear laughter. To no longer feel alone in the knotted mystery of life.

⸺

One night in an Irish pub, over dinner with writer Brian Doyle, I talked about my newly discovered work, drawing stories forth from people and towns and organizations. "You're a *seanachie*," he declared. Seanachie, he explained, is a Gaelic word meaning "storycatcher." In traditional Irish towns, a storycatcher's role was to unearth, gather, and share stories to strengthen and bind people to one another.

After Brian's declaration, I began to claim my vocation as a storycatcher. I learned to ask questions that drew forth memories: A sacred place from childhood. A memorable winter. A sacrifice. A missed opportunity. I learned to listen for patterns, for change, for the revealing heat of emotion. I read books by writers, oral historians, and professional storytellers and noted how they went about their craft. Over time I learned the warp and woof of stories, how they gather, arch, spiral, and spring forth. I learned how to root up the deepest stories from people and communities, how to catch their scent, how to ferret them out from the tangle of a person's living.

I discovered that in every town the stories wait, like seeds beneath the concrete. They wait within the receptionist who sailed alone across the Black Sea, within the store manager who raised his two sisters after their mother died, within the well-dressed grandmother who spent her youth stealing horses in Saskatchewan. Lower me down into a seemingly empty, colorless place—a fast-food restaurant, a warehouse chain store, a gray office cubicle—and I will excavate a story that will break your heart, a true story that will bust your sides with laughter or unlock all that's bound up in you, a story that will aim you like the North Star toward whatever is true and right. Give me a few hours of your time and I will mirror back a story from your life that will fill you with self-compassion. There's no need to make anything up, no need for fiction. The truth waits to be told, but few know how to catch it. And fewer still know how to tell it.

Each of us wants to catch the birdsong of our own life, but often we need a listener to score the melody, to sing it back to us, to help us whistle forth our own merry tune. It requires certain sensibilities. Presence. Acceptance. Patience. I have to set loose my compassionate imagination. I have to be a vulnerable listener. I have to allow my own fears and wounds to be accessible, touched, made known within the listening.

As a storycatcher, I work to hear the pattern. I try to tune my ear for the drive, the struggle, the change. I listen for desire, for obstacles, for a moment of resolution and peace. I listen for the crossroads when a person found themselves bereft and bewildered and chose to go forward anyhow rather than return to what had always been.

Often the stories I find, the stories that long to be told, are about suffering—the surprise of suffering, the chaos of suffering, the absurdity of suffering, and, ultimately, the transformation of suffering into some redeeming good. My job is to bear witness, to trust the person in front of me (sometimes more than they trust themselves), to validate their wisdom, to delight in their unique genius. My job is to accept, without judgment, that they've done the best they can with the life they've been given.

I have to listen for where the story is coming from. Is it from a wound? Some inner need for attention? Is it fear? A listener receives the story from the same place it is told, so I try to notice where it lands in me. If it comes from cleverness, my brain will take note. If it comes from the gut, it will awaken my compassion or draw laughter from the belly. If it comes from fear, I often find myself anxious, judging, comparing. If it comes from neediness, my body tightens with resistance. If it comes from the heart, tears will gather at my eyes.

I try to listen to what is said and what isn't said. I listen to the silences, the words mumbled and tossed aside. Often the first story someone tells me is not the story they long to tell. The first story is what got them in the door while the real story waits in the car. The first story is crafted to entertain, to please, to get a laugh, to grab attention. But behind that story, waiting in the wings, is the Truth, the real story they long to tell. This is the work of the storycatcher—to hear the unspoken story and invite it out into the open.

———

The theme was Wilderness Tales. Tresa was a high school counselor and one of the six storytellers presenting at the upcoming Hearth. She needed help crafting her story about a cross-country canoe trip. The story began on the Oregon coast where she had lived with her fiancé for two years. He wanted her to meet his parents before the wedding. The parents lived in Michigan. An avid outdoorsman, her fiancé decided they should travel to Michigan by canoe.

For the next hour I listened as she described, in excruciating detail, the landscapes, weather patterns, flora and fauna along the canoe trip. Waterfalls flowing into the Columbia River. Churning rapids of the Missouri. Birds. Sunsets. A lightning storm outside of Chicago. Her story was hardly a "story." Nothing happened. Just one postcard picture after another. I waited.

They leave Chicago and make their way into the interior of Michigan. They paddle up to her future in-laws' home. She meets the parents. They have a party. The End.

I was bored, restless. I felt as if I had been forced to watch someone's vacation videos. Grasping, I asked, "So then you got married?"

"Well, no."

"Why not?"

"Well, it was because of a hamburger. I wanted a hamburger, and he said, 'No.'"

Suddenly, I was interested. "Tell me about the hamburger."

Bit by bit, with patience and gentle questions, I heard the story hiding behind the story. She came from a long line of abusive relationships. Her grandfather beat her grandmother. Her father beat her mother. As a young adult she found herself in a similarly volatile relationship. She was actually terrified of canoeing to Michigan, did not want to go, but she was afraid to contradict her partner. Forced to paddle for hours upon hours, she became physically strong for the first time in her life. Canoeing through rain, thunder, and windstorms, she began to face her fears and develop some psychological strength. When they entered the headwaters of the Mississippi River, a local told them to stop at a riverside restaurant for the best hamburger in the region.

It was at that point she did something she had never seen a woman in her family do—she asked a man for something she desired. "I want to stop and get one of those hamburgers." Her fiancé initially agreed, but when the riverbank restaurant came into view, he changed his mind and they continued down river. "It was at that point I made a decision that I would leave this man, no matter what it took, and start my life over."

Anticipating the night Tresa would tell her story, she asked her adult children to fly home to hear it. Her story opened like this: "There were three rules passed down from the women in my family. One, a man will always be the captain of your life. Two, your needs will always be subordinate to his needs. Three, don't rock the boat." Her story went from a pastoral picture book to the inspiring testimony of a woman who found her strength and freedom amid the heartbreaking wilderness of generational abuse.

We are mysteries unto ourselves. Our lives come to us in random moments, and we do our best to string them together with desire—desire fulfilled, desire thwarted, longings aching to be realized. Listen to the stories you tell others. The stories you repeat. The stories you want told at the end of your life. What does the story want from the listeners? What is it you need others to understand? Listen to the story your sister repeats again and again. What is it she wants from you? What is the reaction she seeks to evoke? Admiration? Empathy? Righteous anger? Gratitude? What is the unmet longing, the wound untended, the fear that seeks comfort? What is the story beneath the story? The one she isn't telling but needs you to hear?

The poet Mary Oliver spent over forty years with her partner, Molly Malone Cook. Thirty years into their relationship, while reading in an upstairs room, Oliver heard her lover whistling a jaunty tune in the downstairs kitchen. In thirty years of companionship, she had never heard her whistle a note. Now an unexpected melodious tune emanated from the kitchen. Oliver expressed her bewilderment, "Who is this I've been living with for thirty years? / This clear, dark, lovely whistler?"

None of us are as we appear. Almost every story we tell of ourselves is too small. No matter how epic, most stories seek to reduce, explain, control. They leave something out in the telling. The long periods of time stuck, confused, bored. The contradictory actions and feelings that make us appear fuzzy and untrustworthy. We tend to live in the in-between, the space between the story we tell and the story we are actually living. The work is to integrate the two.

Let the living tell the story. Let the story harvest what is most true and useful. This is the job of the storycatcher. To mind the disparity between story and experience. To mirror what has been lived back to the person who has lived it. To help a person feel the shape of their own soul and whistle it blessed.

8

UNDOCUMENTED STORIES

There's a reason we do not take the time to listen to those who are suffering. To listen to the stories of the vulnerable is to become vulnerable. To hear the stories of the helpless is to be reminded of our own human frailty. To listen openly to those in need is to feel responsible for their well-being. To hear the truth of another person's struggle is to make us open to pain. The only way to keep ourselves protected, safe from empathizing with another person, is by refusing to hear their story. Otherwise, we may be tempted to care, tempted to respond, tempted to change, tempted to remember: They are just like me.

———

It's a Saturday morning, seven weeks after Donald Trump is sworn in as POTUS. I am in Austin, Texas, with Guatemala-born activist Monica Tornoe, driving to a high school where a free legal clinic is being offered to local immigrants.

We arrive thirty minutes before the clinic is set to open, and already there is a line of fifty or so Hispanic families waiting quietly at the cafeteria door. The people are somber, the air thick with anxiety. Law students and professors seated at tables with various handouts in Spanish are helping people understand their rights in the face of the deportation threats. We've been told by Justin Estep, the clinic coordinator, that most people who come to the clinic are undocumented and will be told they have no real protection. "It's heartbreaking," he tells us. "Families come to us pleading for assistance, but there really isn't much we can do."

Monica has asked me to help find a way to share the stories of the undocumented. The plan is simple and straightforward: We post signs and spread flyers inviting people to sit and handwrite their stories anonymously. We set up a table near the exit with paper, pens, and clipboards. We inform people that their writings will be collected and displayed as part of a traveling gallery designed to magnify their voices and hopefully help change the narrative about who they are and why they are here.

By the time the clinic opens, the line has tripled in length. Monica and I stand and wait to talk with people as they leave. Some are in tears. Others look deeply tired, burdened, and weighted with worry. Many are dressed for work. Some have their children with them. We offer water and a place to sit. Although some are wary and others too pained to write, a handful of people eventually put pen to paper. Sometimes a family gathers around and quietly reads over the shoulder as a parent or spouse writes. Some parents speak their story out loud while their teenage son or daughter transcribes. Some children have not fully understood the story of their parent, and there are tearful conversations as they comprehend their family's situation.

The whole process is deeply uncomfortable. I find myself apologizing to people, hoping to assuage some of my own guilt, mitigate the disparity. Monica, however, will not let me off the hook. Half-joking, she continually cajoles me, "You need to use your white privilege to get some media coverage." "We are running out of pens. Take your white male privilege to Office Depot and get us some free pens."

That afternoon a film crew from Germany happens to be doing a documentary on Austin's South by Southwest festival. Monica spots them near the school, takes me by the arm, and walks me over to the producer. "Use your white privilege to get us some international coverage." Five-foot-one Monica then stands smiling, arms folded, while I tell the crew about the stories we're gathering from immigrant families. My white privilege works. The producer is intrigued. He talks to me about developing a different storyline on Austin and the festival. He then spends almost an hour interviewing Monica and some of the undocumented families.

We return to the clinics throughout that spring and eventually collect one hundred handwritten stories from undocumented immigrants. Monica carefully translates all the stories into English to be publicly displayed.

I ask her what she hears in the stories. Monica closes her eyes and takes a deep breath. "Weeping. They are weeping and pleading for mercy."

———

So many of our modern interactions with suffering people involve listening and not responding. Watching, seeing, and not acting. Seeing, hearing, and then going to sleep. We are biologically wired to respond to suffering. Throughout history we have celebrated stories of people who act on behalf of others. We admire and honor people who right wrongs. But here we sit.

Stories are designed to move us, to inspire us to act. Stories transmit emotions. The etymology of the word *emotion* is "to move out." What happens to our spirits, our psyches, when we hold up stories about the heroically compassionate while we ourselves sit by, passively watching? What happens to our souls when Black neighbors are unjustly killed over and over and over again while we do nothing?

My hunch is that absorbing stories of suffering and injustice without responding eventually conditions us to ignore our natural instincts to care. Over time, many of us grow numb to the empathy we naturally had as children—to feel sorrow for someone in need, to comfort and aid those who are hurting, to act when witnessing injustice. After hours upon hours of sitting and listening, we can forget that the purpose of the moral stories we venerate is to get us moving, to stir up our deepest and most sacred impulses to love, to care, to right the wrongs. If we rarely exercise our ability to actually, concretely help someone, our spiritual impulses atrophy and we become less alive, less awake, less ourselves. Over time, our heart recedes and shrinks. Our compassionate imagination dims. Our receptors for love curl inward.

On a balmy June evening I am driving through East Austin looking for the home of Carmen Zuvieta. The setting sun is a creamsicle whose orange light melts across the stucco houses. I wind through various neighborhoods until I find the address and park the car. Next door, two women sit in lawn chairs laughing while their men converse in low tones beneath the hood of a truck. Across the street ranchera music plays through an open door while a group of children dance around a sprinkler. Thirty-five percent of Austin's population is Hispanic. So much of Texas's food, art, and music is influenced by Latin culture, yet rarely are its Hispanic neighbors' stories heard.

It is my job to find and prepare storytellers for an evening at Austin's Mexican American Cultural Center. The event is titled "Breaking Down Walls," and the hope is that the gathering will magnify the stories of local immigrants and give the media access to their voices. I knock, and a six-year-old boy with short-clipped hair and black-rimmed glasses opens the door. He smiles broadly and, without taking his eyes off me, yells, "Mama!" The home is modest, the walls bare, the front room sparsely furnished. Carmen and I sit facing one another in the family room while Emmanuel jumps up and down on a loveseat like it's a trampoline. The boy smiles and jumps, showing me how high he can go. He reminds me of my own sons at this age.

Silvia, Carmen's eighteen-year-old daughter, enters the room while texting on her phone. Carmen's English is not well-developed, so she has asked her daughter to help translate. Silvia looks up, says hello, then attends to her phone. "Sit down," she tells her brother calmly who is jumping two or three feet above the couch while making various gymnastic twists. Still texting, Silvia explains, "He misses his dad. He needs a man around here." The boy obeys his sister, and Silvia hands him some sort of electronic device. As her son settles, Carmen looks at me and begins speaking. Silvia finds a kitchen chair, puts her phone in her pocket, and sits next to her mother. Then, in even, somber tones, she begins to translate her mother's words.

Carmen has lived in the United States for over twenty years. Her children are all American citizens, and she herself was granted permanent residency. But four years ago, her husband was deported. The heartbreak of losing her husband and the difficulty of working and raising children as a single parent have been extremely hard. Carmen works multiple jobs to pay the bills, but she uses much of her free time working to change laws that unfairly criminalize immigrants and their families. Carmen has a powerful presence. She knows the truth and is not afraid to speak it. "America wants our bodies but does not want us."

For an hour I listen while her daughter translates. I am listening for the storyline when suddenly, during a pause, Silvia speaks to me directly. "You know, when politicians talk about deporting people, they rarely think of the children left behind. Deporting my father means they are harming American children." Like her mother, Silvia has a powerful emotional presence. Carmen and I both turn and give her our full attention. I take my audio recorder and direct it toward her.

Silvia pauses, closes her eyes, and then begins with an image. She is eight years old, standing in front of her elementary school, anxiously searching the lineup of cars. She is wondering if she has been orphaned, worried this might be the day her parents, who she calls her "sun and moon," will disappear. She completes the image and then looks me in the eye. "That was how every school day of my childhood ended."

Silvia is a natural storyteller. She paints a second picture. Her father is put in jail by immigration officials after a small car accident. She is ten years old. She visits her father in jail. Cold fluorescent lights. The peeling walls a sickly green. Her father thin, pale. She remembers crying. Arms outstretched, her hands against the plexiglass. Unable to reach him.

The family spends whatever money they have on lawyers. Carmen works hard to pay the bills while raising three children. And then one day in February, in her thirteenth year, Silvia's aunt picks her up from school. "Where's

Mom?" she asks. Her fears come true. Her father has been deported.

Her family is no longer a family. Her house is no longer a home. Eventually, they are able to call their father in Mexico. "I don't remember any of us speaking. All we did was cry."

Silvia's younger brother is two when their father is taken. "Every time he heard a car he would run and open the front door, hoping to see Papa. We would tell him, 'Papa is not coming home,' but he didn't want to believe us. Ten minutes later he would hear a car and run to the door again." I look over at Emmanuel. I know he hears us, but his face remains concentrated on the game he is playing.

Silvia finishes talking and her brother comes over and sits on her lap, his face still focused on the video screen. It is clear to me that she should be the one to share her story. I turn to Carmen. "I think your daughter has a story to tell." Carmen doesn't need translation. She nods her head and says to me in English, "Yes. She is the one." I turn off my recorder and pack up my notes. Silvia and I agree to talk again to hone her story for the event.

Carmen walks me to the door and just as I start to leave, Emmanuel scoots around his mother, stands in front of me, and holds out his hand to say goodbye. It is a formal gesture, a grown-up gesture. I shake his hand, but when I try to speak to him, my voice catches in my throat. I look at Carmen, helpless. "It's okay," she says comfortingly. "It's okay."

She puts her hand on Emmanuel's shoulder and pulls him close. I turn and head for the car.

———

On the way home I think back to a day I spent at an unregulated refugee camp in Calais, France. The camp held more than five thousand people, almost all young men, from Sudan, Iraq, Somalia, Pakistan, Afghanistan, and other countries suffering from war and poverty. I had helped deliver food and medical supplies and then spent much of my time taking photos and collecting stories. I remember within thirty minutes of arriving at the camp, I wanted to leave. The food and supplies we had brought felt pitiful, so small, so little in contrast to the great need. The despair felt impermeable, the young men ghostlike, aimless, stranded, in need of friendship and care. I spent the day talking with various refugees. Eager to be heard, the young men gathered around me and, one by one, told me their stories while I worked to offer the only real thing I could offer—presence.

When the day came to a close, we walked back to our vans. I felt emotionally exhausted, relieved to be leaving. But then, just as we buckled our seatbelts, two young men, no more than twenty years old, tapped on my friend Peter's window. They both looked defeated, desperate. In broken English one of them said, "Can we go? Go with you?" Peter smiled sorrowfully, explained we didn't have any seats and were headed back to the United Kingdom.

The men stood staring. There was a pause, and then, wanting to help, Peter asked, "Where are you headed?" They shrugged their shoulders, searched for words, then one of them said, "Anywhere." All four of us went silent. And in that silence the chasm was felt.

Peter looked over at me, his face pained. He turned back to the two young men and spoke the hard truth, "I'm sorry, lads. I'm sorry. We're headed back. I can't take you." The two young men, unsurprised by this response, nodded their heads. Then they stepped back from the van, raised their hands, and started waving.

As the van backed away, I raised my hand. I held it up and waved at these two defeated young men. I waved, and they waved back. A line came to me from a Stevie Smith poem:

> not waving
> but drowning.

———

Austin is hot and muggy as the end of June approaches. Monica and I are working tirelessly to promote the storytelling event. As instructed, I try to use my white privilege to get some media attention. Eventually a few local papers and radio stations call us to do interviews. The event spreads across social media. National Public Radio's immigration correspondent sends word he will be attending.

On the night of the event, the staff at the Mexican American Cultural Center is concerned that ICE might raid the gathering since some of the storytellers have been publicized as undocumented. I talk with Patricia, one of our storytellers who is at risk of such seizure. "I told my children that if ICE comes and takes me away, don't be afraid," she tells me. "Be strong. We are not going to live in fear." In the courtyard of the building are the handwritten stories of the undocumented. Like clothes hung to dry, they are fastened on lengths of twine with tiny wooden clips.

Inside the building there is a black stage and seating for three hundred. The auditorium fills quickly, and the staff searches for extra chairs to fill the open spaces. When chairs run out, people sit on the floor at the edge of the stage. Some stand against the wall. It is the largest event anyone can remember hosting in the building. The evening begins with live music from Ecuadorian, Peruvian, Mexican, and Colombian folk singers, and then our storytellers take the stage.

Twenty-three-year-old Alex, who has spent half his life in Mexico and half in the United States, compares the two worlds. In America, he has been called racial slurs like "spic" and "wetback." But when he's in Mexico, he is teased for being too American. His friends called him a gringo—tell him he is too "square, unemotional, a workaholic, just like all Americans." His story is about navigating the prejudices of both cultures while trying to maintain his identity. "At the heart," he says, "we are not our labels. At heart, we are all the same."

Julieta is the second storyteller. She became an activist in high school. She helped form the Dreamers, a lobbying group for the rights of immigrants who were brought here as children. She travels to Washington, DC, and meets with congressional leaders. "I was only seventeen at the time, but I would look at each of these powerful men and ask them, 'Why are you sending me to a country I've never known?'"

Cynthya is the next teller. She shares her childhood dream of becoming a lawyer, the pain when she realized she did not share the same rights as her friends, the heartbreak when she was told her legal status prevented her from seeking employment and receiving financial aid for attending university. The other tellers share similar stories of thwarted dreams, and the disorientation in facing criminalization simply for trying to live and survive.

One of the last storytellers is Silvia. Her mother, Carmen, and brother, Emmanuel, are in the audience. It is intimidating to speak to such a large crowd, particularly when you are sharing something so intimate and vulnerable. But Silvia has her mother's strength, and she has learned to claim what she has suffered in a way that gives her authority and power. She tells her story well: The loving and playful family. The debilitating anxiety as a young girl. Her father's arrest. The legal fight. The battle against depression. The work to transform her pain into activism on behalf of others.

She ends her story with images from her graduation. The pride in finishing high school. The pain at the absence of her father. She closes with a moment after the ceremony when her mother, siblings, and extended family gather for pictures. At one point her older cousin pulls her aside and says to her, "I'm so proud of you, Silvia. Not because you graduated—I always knew you would graduate. I am proud of you because you survived."

———

At the end of the storytelling event, the NPR reporter pulls me aside and asks if he can contact the storytellers. "We need to hear more of these stories and less from politicians and analysts." In the following months, he records interviews with some of the storytellers and broadcasts not only their experiences but also their impressions of national immigration policies.

Moved by the stories of undocumented residents, administrators at the University of Texas display the gallery of handwritten stories within their law and medical schools to increase empathy and understanding. Then they invite some of the undocumented storytellers to share their experiences at a public forum. The gallery and video recordings of the live storytelling event continue to tour various locations throughout Austin and beyond.

Often the measure of a person can be assessed by the stories they tell and the values they hold toward the immigrant, the outsider, the stranger. Our past president Donald Trump referred to the people of Latin America as rapists, snakes, and thugs—fabricating or exaggerating stories about the crimes committed by immigrants. Listening to fear-based, one-sided stories not only affects our thoughts on immigration but also trains our brains and bodies to feel defensive and threatened. Studies show that hearing these stories causes the brain to release cortisol, sometimes called "the stress hormone," which directs our jaws to clench, stomachs to tighten, hearts to race. Neuropathways are built that associate immigrants with danger and repulsion. Once the brain is trained, we can feel threatened every time we see someone who "looks like" an immigrant. Never mind that many of the stories are unfounded; once they have burrowed a network of neuropathways within us, it is difficult to perceive any facts that counter the stories we've heard.

It is possible, however, to retrain the body. One of the best ways to rewire the brain is by gathering together and sharing a different story—a more human story that avoids labels and stereotypes. An honest story that reminds the human heart of the basic struggle to live with dignity. One of the ways we counter prejudice is by offering a space where people can tell their own true stories, their own grassroot struggles. We are freed or imprisoned, connected or isolated by the stories we tell one another. To expose ourselves to another human's journey is to not only hear the ground truth but also to allow our hearts to soften and our minds to open so that we can access greater empathy, compassion, and trust. So that we can offer the same hospitality to others that we ourselves long to receive.

9

TRAGEDY

On October 1, 2015, a twenty-six-year-old student at Umpqua Community College (UCC) walked into his morning writing and composition class and began shooting. Ten minutes later the instructor, eight students, and the shooter were dead. Nine additional students were wounded, some of them critically, and hundreds of staff and students were left traumatized. It was the largest mass shooting in Oregon's modern history.

The story of a school shooting in America, sadly, is unoriginal. Students and teachers gathered to learn, to grow, to discover the wonders of living—suddenly shot to death by a fellow student. Unnecessary, unwarranted, and, horrifyingly, heartbreakingly repetitive. But it is a story we seem cursed to live through again and again and again and again.

A week after the UCC shooting, I received a phone call from my friend Max Gimbel. Max lives near UCC and works for a foundation that serves rural towns across Oregon. I listened as he told me of the collective shock and trauma he witnessed among his friends and coworkers, as well as the sudden outpouring of care and generosity. I listened and then he came to the purpose of his call: "How can you help?"

How does a community heal from trauma? How does it recover trust after such a fundamental betrayal? Often our resiliency, our capacity to heal, depends on the stories we form and share in the wake of tragedy. *This is what happened to us. This is how we felt. This is what it means to us now.* When we're invited to share our experience with others, we work to create something whole out of the physical and psychological wreckage.

The stories composed by the national media in the days following the tragedy were wearily familiar. Gun rights versus gun restrictions. The decline of mental health services. Tragic (at times exploitive) profiles of victims. The stories did not reflect the intimate, personal loss that people across Douglas County and beyond were feeling. The victims were not simply characters in a poignant national news story. Those killed and injured were friends from church, children of coworkers, teammates from softball, weekend fishing buddies. The media stories also did not capture the sudden upswell of generosity, the way the community came together to comfort those suffering. One resident told me,

"If I sat and listened to the national news, I would have no idea they were describing the town where I lived."

So we decided to look for a way to empower local people to share their own stories of the tragedy. With input from college administrators, students, and various community groups, Max, his colleagues, and I developed the Umpqua Story Project. The project's mission would be to facilitate healing through sharing stories.

Umpqua Community College sits on a lovely hundred-acre campus that borders the North Umpqua River. The college is the center of social life for many of the 106,000 residents of Douglas County. It's the primary venue for concerts, theater, and other cultural events. Locals gather at the college for swim lessons, concerts, driving school, SAT exams, vocational certification, weddings, and other rites of passage. UCC is just over a hundred miles from where I live and only ten miles from where my wife grew up. My wife's high school held its graduation at the college. As a young girl she saw her first plays and musicals with her family in the college auditorium.

I arrived at the empty campus around ten o'clock in the evening. The campus was still, insulated in a fluorescent fog lit by the many parking and security lights. The modular classroom where the shooting took place was ominously shrouded in black plastic with yellow caution tape staked at the perimeter. I parked and stepped out of my car. Immediately, a security guard pulled alongside me in a golf cart. "The campus is closed," he announced. When I told the guard my assignment, he relaxed and stepped out from the cart. "You know my son played on the soccer team with one of the victims? They grew up together." His voice caught with emotion and he turned away. "Here. Come with me. I'll take you inside."

We walked in silence to the glossy black tent that had been constructed around the shooting site. He turned on a flashlight, pulled aside an opening in the tarp, and we walked onto the cemented walkway that bordered the building. He stopped in front of a classroom door. "This is the room." I noticed roses taped to the wall just outside the door. The guard told me that Chris Mintz, one of the students wounded in the shooting, had placed the roses that day. Mintz was one of the heroes. A young father and Iraq war veteran, he had run toward the shooting rather than away. After directing students in nearby classes to evacuate, he placed his body against the door of the classroom to keep the shooter from exiting. Within moments the shooter ran around through a side door and confronted Mintz. Face to face with the shooter, Mintz asked for mercy, saying, "It's my son's birthday." He was shot five times. Miraculously, none of the wounds were fatal. Released from the hospital, Mintz returned to the site with ten flowers, nine white for the victims and one red rose.

"What's the red rose for?" I asked.

"He put it there for the shooter."

We were silent for a moment, both of us staring at the single red rose. Then the guard said, "Kind of boggles the mind that he wanted to remember him."

———

Sometimes a story can kindle murderous rage, or crystallize resentment, or summon hatred instead of empathy. It might be a story called *Race Determines Worth*. A story titled *Killing Is Holy*. The young man who shot and killed his teacher and eight other students fed himself on a story he called *The Most Hated Person in the World*. It was a story he constructed about himself inspired by the writings of other mass shooters. It was a story that, to him and other hurting, angry, socially isolated young men, was a story of martyrdom: the scorned, friendless boy enacts just revenge on those who have ignored him, willingly sacrificing his own life in a valiant quest for attention. The story is self-absorbed, narcissistic, destructive, and utterly delusional. And yet it is a story that lives because it somehow gives expression to the anger these young men feel.

As I worked in Roseburg and felt the terrible, needless suffering caused by one person, I couldn't help but wonder: What if the shooter had been given other stories that helped him express the hurt he felt? What if he had been told stories by groups of men who had transformed their own pain and alienation, men who had found friendship and community through heroic acts of service? I wondered about the story this shooter and other violent young men are communicating about our society, about growing up male, about the ways men are formed.

———

Early on a Saturday morning that fall, a group of twenty volunteers gathered at the Douglas County Museum. They were mostly retirees, people who had time, people who knew something about suffering. They had responded to a public appeal for "compassionate listeners." After some training in active listening skills and story collection, they were ready to be deployed.

We handed out signs, pens, paper, and audio recording equipment. The compassionate listeners stationed themselves at various coffee shops, libraries, churches, schools, downtown sidewalks, and other public spaces. There they sat patiently, humbly, grandparently, next to signs that read, "Share your story of October 1." For nine months, these compassionate listeners spent hundreds of hours collecting stories from the public. Sometimes they brought warm drinks and homemade cookies. Other times they sat with their knitting or crossword puzzles. From time to time someone would sit, sometimes just for the cookie and coffee, sometimes out of curiosity, sometimes to relieve a burden. The listeners would welcome them, make small talk, and then, when the person was comfortable, their story would begin. "My daughter was at the school when the shooting took place . . ."

The stories often came in pieces. The end first. Now the beginning. Then a sudden memory from twenty years back.

Now a description of an encounter from yesterday. The survivor is the teacher, oral historians have often said. And so the listener must stay curious, open. *Let the teacher teach.*

Sometimes a person preferred to write their story. Sometimes they wanted a memory recorded. All the while the compassionate listener sought to be hospitable, their face, posture, spirit communicating: *I'm glad you're here. Your story matters. Take as much time as you need.* When the telling ended, the listener thanked them for their story. Sometimes they hugged or shook hands. And then the teller departed. A little less alone.

Six months into the project, we received an email from a parent of one of the victims. "What about *our* story?" I called the mother, and she told me about a recent experience while grocery shopping. On the way back to her car, there was a parked van with an enlarged photo of her son and the other victims taped to the doors. A handmade sign read, "Never forget."

The mother became emotional. "All these strangers posting pictures of my son. Newspapers and television telling the story of my son. They did not know him. He was much more than a shooting victim. When does his story get to be told by those who knew him?"

I felt terrible. Why had we not tried harder to reach out to the families of the victims? I apologized to the mother and said, "I have a son the same age as your son. I cannot imagine what you are going through."

"Yes, you can," she said. "You just don't want to."

And maybe that was it. I was afraid of the grief, afraid of the meaninglessness. Some primal, protective instinct steered me away from the suffering. I wanted to keep my distance from the horror these families were experiencing.

Over the next few months we met with families who wanted to tell the story of their lost or injured loved one. Sometimes it was a parent or two; other times a whole family gathered. We set up recording equipment and listened. There were many, many tears—accompanied by a kind of bottomless grief. There were also smiles, funny stories, moments of wonder and gratitude. Memories were shared, loved ones brought back to life through words and stories. We thanked the families for sharing, then with their permission, carefully archived their memories in the local museum so people could come to know how much those lost were deeply wronged, how much they deserved to live, how much they were loved by the friends and families who remain.

———

Within human beings lies a desire to serve, to respond compassionately to the needs of others. Sometimes it is latent. Sometimes it is only realized in an emergency. In the days and weeks after the tragedy, Max and his colleagues noticed a transformation within the local community. The barriers between people softened. In the grocery line, at sporting events, in schools and workplaces, there was a discernible shift—people were more patient with one another, more kind. In the wake of the pain and terror, there seemed to be a greater sense of unity, of meaning and shared purpose.

Restaurants organized meals for victim families and first responders. The high school band played weekends on street corners to raise money. Coffeehouses gave out free drinks. Therapists offered free counseling. Bars contributed nightly profits to victim families. T-shirts and stickers were made and given away. Students set up car washes to help cover medical expenses for the injured. Musicians visited the hospital each night to play. A fishing derby was organized to help cover funeral expenses. Businesses posted signs of prayer and encouragement. A group of waitresses quietly donated their wages. People offered their gifts to help those who had suffered. Hats were passed. Money was raised. Churches and counseling centers and places of care were opened all hours. In response to one person's act of violence, a community offered a hundred acts of love.

We documented these stories of generosity in the hope of forming a communal memory, a touchstone of social possibility, a reminder of how people could live together long after the tragedy subsided. In *Paradise in Hell*, author Rebecca Solnit explains that we are trained to fear "the public" and mistrust our neighbors, to live concerned only with our private, personal well-being. But when an emergency hits, when social structures break down, when the world falls apart, communities discover a yearning and capacity to care for one another. "Horrible in itself, disaster is sometimes a door back into paradise, the paradise at least in which we are who we hope to be, do the work we desire, and are each our sister's and brother's keeper."

———

The stories remembered within a community can either separate us through fear, mistrust, and resentment or bind us with empathy, generosity, and self-sacrifice. The stories we tell often mirror the values we hold and the world we seek to create. One year after the shooting, we produced a gallery of written stories, audio recordings, and photographs reflecting the many individual and communal acts of generosity and kindness. The collection was shared at Umpqua Community College, and on the opening night, we invited the public to come and hear six local community members present their experience of the local response to the shooting tragedy.

Artist Susan Rochester remembered filling her truck full of art supplies and driving to campus when she heard the news. She described how students, staff, and neighbors gathered to paint memorials to friends, draw images of hope, sculpt the grief and loss they felt. Andrea Zielinski, the volunteer coordinator for the Douglas County sheriff's office, recalled the particular suffering of first responders. She told stories of how volunteers from various government agencies gave time to help her answer phones, provide meals, and care for the families of law enforcement officers working overtime. Pub owner Casey O'Toole remembered a night when breweries donated beer, distributors covered food expenses, and community members volunteered shifts to raise funds for victim families. O'Toole remembered one local couple who was in San Francisco on the night of the pub fundraiser. Waking up in an oceanfront hotel, preparing to celebrate their fiftieth wedding anniversary, it suddenly struck them that they were in the wrong place. They promptly canceled the rest of their trip and drove back to Roseburg, where they spent the evening washing dishes and waiting tables to help raise funds.

Justin Troxel recalled weeping with strangers when he heard a police scanner directing all ambulances in the county to Umpqua Community College. Looking for a way to respond, he gathered friends together and began crafting metal signs shaped into the state of Oregon with a heart cut out over Douglas County. He sold fifty signs within the first hour of posting them online and donated all the proceeds to victims' families. People all across Oregon and the United States sent in orders. Each night, dozens of people gathered at Justin's home to help process orders, collect money, paint and mail out signs. In just two months, Justin and his neighbors raised more than $135,000 for those affected by the shooting.

Kelly Wright, the victim's advocate at the Douglas County District Attorney's office, shared a collection of moments when the victims' families offered her care in the midst of their own grief and loss. As she recalled, "The families that suffered from this tragedy not only became my family but also a source of strength for one another." The evening ended with a story from Dustin Cosby, a photographer and instructor at the college who helped facilitate a spontaneous community vigil the night after the tragedy. He described what it was like when so many people brought instruments, candles, chairs, blankets, food, and drinks to create the vigil and support affected families. "It was an evening when thousands of people gathered together, saying, 'Here I am. I want to help. Here's what I can give.'"

———

We are made from the stories we've been told, the stories we tell ourselves, and the stories we tell one another. The world can be terrifying, wonderful, repulsive, wounding, comforting—sometimes all at once. The stories we are fed often determine how we live amid the contradictions. Stories can expand the boundaries of the heart to hold the chaos, the betrayals, the destructive absurdities with a sense of grace, resiliency, and moral courage. Or they can shrink us to become brittle, fearful, destructive. We need a comforting space and compassionate ears to sort out what we have suffered, to find the stories that recover and repair the world, to keep our hearts intact.

On October 1, 2015, a troubled young man entered a classroom at Umpqua Community College killing nine people and wounding nine others. Those acts sent out a shockwave of pain and sorrow throughout Douglas County.

But that is only one part of the story.

The larger story is that those lost and wounded are loved. The larger story is that the people of Douglas County grew closer. The larger story, as one community member shared, is that "in the midst of suffering, we discovered something we always knew but rarely said. We belong to one another."

INTERLUDE

SHOES

The Three Little Birds Café sits in the old mercantile building in the historic town of Fort Jones, California. Fewer than seven hundred people live within this narrow valley, which once served as a stagecoach stop for travelers on their way to Oregon. On one dusky June evening the café is full of locals, many in cowboy hats and boots. On the back wall a metal loading door opens up, revealing neglected acres of high grass and star thistle that disappear into the dark firs of the Siskiyou Mountains.

There is an ease, a familiarity in the room as a white-bearded man plays steel guitar and croons Tom Waits's "Looking for the Heart of Saturday Night." The theme for the evening is "How I Spent My Summer Vacation," and people are gathered to share stories as a fundraiser for the local family health center. One by one, the high school theater teacher invites various people up front to share their tales—a summer spent at sea, a camp romance, losing a tour group in Rome. Toward the end of the evening, Angela West, a young woman known by many in the room, gets up to speak. When it's announced that she has recently graduated from college, the room greets her with whoops and applause.

It began with a summer internship at Washington, DC's, United States Holocaust Memorial Museum. Angela applied, was accepted, and soon relocated to the East Coast. After some classes and train- ing, she was assigned to work in the Permanent Exhibition, which contains artifacts that include photographs, cobblestones from the Warsaw Ghetto, survivors' testimonies, and a full-size rail car used to transport people to Nazi concentration camps. Emotionally, the most powerful room within the Permanent Exhibit is what is referred to as "the shoe room."

The room is a low-lit rectangular space with a narrow cement walkway. The walkway is bordered by four thousand shoes seized from concentration camp prisoners in Majdanek, Poland. Work boots, platform heels, casual flats, sandals, loafers, men's shoes, women's shoes, children's shoes piled nearly two feet deep along the walls of the room.

Many days that summer Angela was assigned to monitor the third floor of the Permanent Exhibition, which included the shoe room. Her role was to assist visitors, answer questions, and provide needed information. She was also there to protect the shoes and other objects. These aging artifacts, especially leather shoes, are fragile and sensitive to oils from human skin, camera flashes, and sunlight. Throughout the exhibit signs and placards instruct visitors to abstain from handling the artifacts. Nevertheless, Angela regularly had to stop people from reaching over the low glass walls to touch the shoes.

Over the summer, Angela became increasingly frustrated. Every single day, she could count on a handful of visitors ignoring the museum's instructions and reaching over the barrier, at times triggering the alarm.

She decided to change tactics and started explaining to visitors the effect of human oils and the importance of not touching such fragile artifacts. These explanations and warnings also went unheeded. Group after group, young and old, tourists from other countries and US citizens would stop, stare, and then some would inevitably reach to touch the shoes.

Near the end of the summer, Angela started to speak quite curtly to visitors. "Please keep your arms and hands away from the glass barriers. There is an alarm, and we cannot touch the shoes." People nodded their heads. They appeared to be listening. Yet still, as if in a trance, they would stop, they would stare, and then they would reach.

During the last week of her internship, Angela was assigned to spend the day working at the museum's warehouse to assist an associate with cleaning and organization. They drove out of Washington, DC, to a nondescript, metal-sheeted building in rural Maryland. They stepped out of the car and walked over to a gray security door. There were no signs, no markings on the door or on the building. Once past the outer entrance and security, they entered a large, temperature-controlled warehouse lined with wide, archival cabinets and bookshelves.

According to the museum associate, only about 10 percent of the artifact collection is on display at the museum. Most of the artifacts are stored in the warehouse. Angela's coworker led her down the aisle of cabinets, stopping to open drawers filled with photographs, diaries, clothing, and sacred objects all donated to the museum by families who suffered the Holocaust.

At one point, Angela opened a drawer labeled Lilly Friedman. Inside was a wedding dress with a remarkable story.

Twenty-one-year-old Lilly Lax was a Holocaust survivor. At the end of the war, she was sent with her sister to a camp for displaced persons in Bergen-Belsen, Germany. While standing in a food distribution line, she met a handsome young man named Ludwig Friedman. Despite the cold, muddy, harsh conditions of the camp, they courted and fell in love. Three weeks later Ludwig asked Lilly to marry him. Lilly's dream was to be married in a white wedding dress. Ludwig took it upon himself to make this dream a reality.

Both Lilly and Ludwig were refugees without money and possessions. Ludwig began to save his coffee and cigarette rations to use as currency. One day a former German air pilot turned up at the camp seeking to trade his parachute for rations. They haggled, and Ludwig exchanged two pounds of coffee and a couple of packages of cigarettes for the parachute. He took the white rayon fabric to the women's barracks, and Lilly found a seamstress who agreed to make a wedding dress. On January 27, 1946, four hundred refugees walked fifteen miles in the snow to the nearest synagogue in the town of Celle, Germany, to attend the wedding. Lilly wore her beautiful white wedding gown. Over the next year, Lilly's sister and at least seventeen other women were married in that same dress.

SHOES

The museum associate finished telling Angela the story and then invited her to ever-so-carefully touch the dress. Angela stood in silence, her fingers lightly grazing the airy, delicate wedding dress that represented the newfound hopes of so many young lovers. She tried to feel the weight of those lives—the heartache, the hope, the longing.

The associate returned, and together they began to work in another area of the warehouse. At one point, Angela found herself standing next to a drawer labeled "Shoes." Angela asked permission to look inside. She gripped the handle of the wide metal drawer and slowly rolled it open. To her surprise, the drawer contained one tiny pair of leather baby shoes.

Angela knew the rules. She had repeated them to museum visitors all summer long. But when she saw those shoes—she reached.

She stretched out her arms and reached. So natural. So honest. So human. Who can keep from reaching?

10

THE APOCALYPSE

One morning my daughter came bursting into my bedroom. "There's a rat in the fireplace!" she shouted. I ran out into the family room, and there up against the fireplace door I could see a small head and black eye pressed against the glass. I slowly opened the door. There was a sudden storm of wings and ashes. It was not a rat. It was a bird, a scrub jay, trapped in the fireplace. Each time I reached to grab it or shoo it out, the bird flapped up into the chimney and perched on the metal flue. I left the door open and waited for the ashes to settle and the bird to fly out, but the bird stayed where it was, just out of reach.

For the next two days the scrub jay suffered in our fireplace, and we along with it. Sometimes during dinner or while playing a board game, we'd hear a sudden thwacking of wings and a cloud of ashes would come pouring out from the fireplace. The ashes must have confused the bird, because it was unable to figure out how to leave. "Help it, Dad!" Gracie would cry. So I tried to help by reaching inside and attempting to usher the jay out from the fireplace. But no luck. The bird would avoid my hands and eventually flutter back up into the chimney and perch. All of us were worried, Gracie especially, that the bird would soon die of dehydration, hunger, or simply by suffocating in the soot.

On the morning of the third day, I went to the fireplace and found the scrub jay leaning weakly against the back bricks, covered in gray ash. Talking as soothingly as I could, I carefully grasped the small bird and carried it to the kitchen sink. I took a damp towel and gently wiped its face and limp body. Then I took it outside and placed it on the ground among the shadowed stems of a hydrangea bush. Gracie joined me and we set down a small cup of water, scattered some sunflower seeds, and then sat on our back deck and quietly watched.

Exhausted and stunned, the bird rested in the shade for an hour or so. Then it sipped some water, pecked a few seeds, and flew off.

———

I sit in a small conference room with Marni Koopman and Tonya Graham, two women who work for the Geos Institute, a nonprofit that assists communities in addressing and adapting to climate change. Marni is a climate change scientist and Tonya is the nonprofit's executive director. They are meeting with me, in part, out of desperation. "Scientists have spent decades showing the public the data on climate change, but there has been little response," Tonya tells me. "We need to tell a better story." I ask them to share the story the science is telling—and then immediately regret asking this question. They present me with a list of charts and statistics prophesizing biological annihilation, ocean acidification, endless floods and fire, the fall of civilization within a hundred years. The scientific data is frighteningly stark: The end of the world as we know it is coming.

"This is the story you're telling?" I ask.

"Yes. How can we make it more inspiring?"

"How about the world doesn't end."

We are small, fragile creatures. Our lives are short. From the perspective of the earth's 4.5 billion years, we humans just got here. None of us meant to cause planetary ruin. Global warming and apocalyptic stories of environmental collapse flood our fragile bodies with foreboding. Fear terrorizes, robs us of the present moment, and dredges up something called climate despair. And despair, according to Buddhist teacher Thich Nhat Hanh, "is the worst thing that can happen to a human being."

Author, screenwriter, and BBC producer John Yorke says that all great stories ask the protagonist one simple question, "Will you revert to your old self and die, or change and live?" One of the gifts of this time is the belated but growing realization that the old story about our relationship to the earth is killing us. Will we revert to the old story that reaps death or change and live? As theologian and environmentalist Martin Palmer says, "We have to story our way out of this."

———

I accept Marni and Tonya's challenge of searching for a story I don't yet know how to tell. I start by listening. I interview researchers at the National Oceanic and Atmospheric Administration. I talk with leading climatologists and environmental activists. In each conversation I hear the same story of catastrophic suffering. "Is there any reason to hope?" I ask. It's an uncomfortable question for many of the scientists who have been trained to simply offer the data as stoically as possible, without opinion, with hardly any adjectives. They all tell me there is hope, but they have little evidence to back this up. And then someone at the National Park Service suggests I talk with Professor Scott Denning, a teacher and climatologist at Colorado State University.

Denning is an atmospheric scientist who has done research for NASA and NOAA and served as the editor for the *Journal of Climate*. In his teaching, Denning had come to the conclusion that the story he and other climatologists were telling only engendered despair. He began to search for a reason to offer hope. He looked for moments in history when human beings have made large-scale, systemic change. He surveyed developments in renewable energy and the economics of phasing out human dependence on fossil fuels. Eventually in his classes and talks to environmental groups, he deliberately ended his presentations with hopeful examples of historical moments when human beings came together to bring about radical change. He then listed the new technological advances that could reduce carbon dioxide and mitigate global warming. He referenced economic models that predict growth in jobs and economic activity as the world switches to renewable sources of energy. He made the convincing case that if we act—if we find the personal, collective, and political will—we can avert the worst suffering of climate change.

I was relieved. Denning's presence and presentation offered some light in the midst of terror. So we hired a videographer and made a short film to be presented to President Obama's task force on climate change. The video ends with Denning talking animatedly about the ways we can address the coming crisis.

There was only one problem. It was still the old story.

According to ecologist Michael Soule, the old story based on data and facts, even when hopeful, can't save us. The old story still treats nature as a commodity with humans as separate consumers. Even if we manage to "fix" global warming, we are still dumping nine billion tons of plastic into the ocean each year. Our rivers are still sick with pesticide run-off. After decades as an ecologist and environmental activist, eighty-year-old Soule claims we need a new story that is rooted and grounded in love. What he's calling for is the same message Indigenous people have been suggesting for centuries: recover our interrelatedness to the natural world; cultivate a reverence for animals, plants, and all living things; seek a sense of equity and balance with nature.

For Soule, telling a new story begins by inviting scientists, conservationists, and environmental activists to step away from the data and talk to people about their love for specific animals, plants, and ecosystems. We need more talk about love and less talk about numbers and disasters, because according to Soule, "we only protect what we love."

Marni, Tonya, and I got together with other environmental and social justice groups and decided to host an entire week of climate change–related events in Ashland, Oregon. One large gathering offered presentations by a number of environmental researchers and scientists to encourage the public to begin working together to address global warming. We knew the data they were going to present was scary, so the night before this gathering, we held a public storytelling event and invited some of the presenters to set aside their professional roles and share a personal story in which we could feel their passion. The hope was that these personal stories would serve as emotional maps that might inspire meaningful action.

Marni, one of the evening's storytellers, began her story in childhood. Growing up as a shy introvert who found joy and aliveness while observing wildlife in natural settings, she felt a great affinity for all animals. In middle school when her friends hung posters of Duran Duran, she pinned up pictures of puffins. She received degrees in environmental studies and ultimately a PhD in ecology. She was offered a prestigious job with the forest service in Colorado, in which she was in charge of reading and summarizing various scientific papers on the effects of climate change on wildlife. Day after day, as she read these very dry scientific reports, a heartbreaking picture began to emerge: Pika, Boreal owls, and mountain goats disappearing throughout the United States; migrating birds flying up from South America only to find the food they relied on had already disappeared; descriptions of auklets dropping out of the sky from starvation.

She read and analyzed thousands of papers, but it wasn't until she came across a particular study on puffins, the animal she had most loved as a child, that she broke down. In a report on seabirds, she read how climate change was forcing the parents of new puffin hatchlings to travel farther and farther in search of food while their chicks starved in their nests. Over a decade, whole colonies of puffins along the coast had disappeared. Marni laid her head on her desk and wept. In her grief, she realized she would need to change. She needed to do something. She could no longer stay at her well-paying desk job. She would need to leave her quiet, introverted life and begin to work with people, to tell them what was happening to the animals and see if she could get people to make a change.

Freed from their scientific straitjackets, most of the storytellers told similar tales of falling in love with Coho

salmon, Alaskan mountains, Oregon rivers, and other particular creatures and spaces. Those of us listening couldn't
help but catch the wonder, delight, and transcendent joy
these scientists experienced as they retold the moments of
connection with the natural world. Similarly, we couldn't
help but feel a shared sense of loss as they described species
disappearing, sea bays emptying, forests burning.

The final story was by Scott Denning, the atmospheric
scientist from Colorado. Scott and his wife received a
phone call in the middle of the night from an ambulance
medic. Scott's sixteen-year-old son had been in a terrible car
accident. The EMT told him to rush to the hospital. Scott
was certain they had made a mistake. It was a school night.
His wife had personally tucked their son into bed just hours
earlier. He hung up the phone and went to his son's bedroom. The bed was empty. The decision was made quickly
that his wife would stay home with their younger child while
Scott went to the hospital. He got dressed and stepped into
the bathroom, his body burning with panic. Although not a
man of faith, in desperation, he directed his attention out-
ward and uttered a kind of prayer. "Whatever is going to
happen, help me be my best self." Suddenly, unexpectedly,
the fear and panic emptied out of his body and he found
himself present. Available. Ready.

He drove through the icy February night and arrived
at the hospital just moments before the ambulance. He
went straight to the emergency entrance. The nurse at the
desk had no knowledge of an accident, no record of his

son. Then two EMTs burst in, pushing a gurney with a boy strapped down. The boy's face was swollen and bloodied. "I did not recognize him and for a brief moment was relieved. This was not my son." But then Scott stepped closer. He looked at the eyes. It was him. The boy was badly injured and barely conscious. He saw his father and started to apologize. Scott dismissed the apologies and offered comfort. And then his son, frightened and in pain, asked, "Dad, am I going to die?"

As present as he could be, as loving as he could be, Scott looked at his son and told him the truth, "I don't know. But I am here. And I love you. And whatever happens, it will be okay."

Day after day, for weeks on end, Scott stayed present with his son in the hospital. Miraculously, his son survived. With a voice full of emotion, Scott then turned to the audience, "Tomorrow you're going to hear presentations about climate change and what is happening to our world. It is serious. It is frightening. But we have to stay present. We have to stay in this together. And we have to bring our best selves. We can't allow fear to overtake us. We have to look at what's happening and respond with love. And it will be okay. It will be okay."

Although each teller conveyed the hard truth of environmental suffering, what emerged from the stories of the scientists was not paralyzing fear and despair. What rose up in that room was love and sorrow. Instead of the doom that climate-change statistics often bear, there was an unexpected sense of comfort in being together, in remembering together, in laughing and marveling and grieving together.

The stories ended, and an appeal was made to support a local climate action group that was fighting to stop a gas pipeline from crossing the state. Buckets were passed, money was donated, petitions were signed, and volunteers were recruited.

The facts had not changed, but we felt them in a new way and were inspired to act in response to the personal journeys of these scientists and environmentalists. And on that evening, if you happened to be in the room, and felt those stories, and joined with your neighbors, you went home a little lighter—hopeful, even.

▬

"They've never built a prison that someone hasn't found a way to break out of."

It was April 1989, and I was a college student conducting an interview with novelist Kurt Vonnegut, while my friend Paul and I drove him to the Portland airport. Vonnegut, the celebrated novelist whose stories of despair and mordant humor often resonated with my own sense of doom. Vonnegut, who had buried the bodies of dead German women and children after they were fire-bombed by US forces in World War II. Vonnegut, whose mother had ended her own life on Mother's Day when he was twenty-one. Vonnegut, who just four years earlier had tried to overdose on sleeping pills.

I was rambling on about nuclear proliferation and troubling signs of environmental destruction, expecting the old man to commiserate when he just smiled and said the thing about prisons. "Isn't it interesting that the streets aren't full of dead bodies every morning?" he added. "I mean, there are so many losers. Almost all of us are losers. But every morning people wake up and say, 'Goddammit, there's got to be a way out of this.'"

In Vonnegut's own stories the world is capricious, chaotic, lonely. I pointed this out to him on our drive and asked if he really felt life was absurd. I had recorded our conversation, and you can hear the resentment in my question. I was twenty-two; Vonnegut was sixty-six. I didn't want to hear that the life left to me by the elders was meaningless. I wanted a different story. Vonnegut sensed my bitterness.

"Do you resent someone telling you the truth? You want me to raise your morale in some way by telling you a story about what we can actually achieve in the future?" He laughed, which then erupted into a smoker's coughing fit.

"But isn't there some middle ground?" I argued.

"Listen. I can't tell you the storm's not coming," he said. "But I can tell you how to weather the storm. What you must do is form an extended family of your own. You will be discontented, you will be deeply unhappy if you try to go through life with too few people around you. If you have fifteen or twenty people, you will survive whatever crisis you experience. Inside you can have courage. You can keep on going, doing what you can. In the coming storm, instead of going after money, go after companionship and community. Because human beings have always survived in extended families. If you go out into the world alone, without any friends, that's like saying, 'Hey, no more vitamin C.' Then your hair falls out and your skin falls off and you're dead. The number one cause of the American malaise is loneliness."

Then Vonnegut went on to tell us stories about prisons and how humans can get out of anything. How they find a way out of every problem. How instead of dying by suicide—which to him seemed a perfectly reasonable choice—humans wake up with a sense of possibility.

We pulled up to the curb of the airport. Vonnegut stepped out of the car and got his bag from the trunk. Then he poked his head back in the passenger-side window, paused, and said, "Hey. Don't give up hope."

We are trained to live in a state of disconnection. We are trained to live in fear. The number of new apocalyptic, end-of-the-world movies keeps increasing. Are we meditating on these stories because we believe the only possible future is chaos, isolation, and death? The antidote to despair is relationship. The antidote to despair is action motivated by love. Might it be possible for us to face the hard changes together? Isn't it possible for us to meet this terribly frightening time with generosity and kindness, with compassion, with humility and remorse, with simple acts of love?

We need to love-story our way out of the apocalypse. We need stories to help us recall something we all knew as children but were trained to forget: That we love this earth. Philosopher and environmental activist Charles Eisenstein recently made a video letter for people despairing over the increasing numbers of fires in the Amazon rainforest. He asked people to imagine themselves ill, suffering on a sickbed, unsure if they really wanted to live. In that situation, he pondered, what conditions give you the will to live? "If people love you. If you're valued. If you have a community. If you're not alone." The earth is on a sickbed, Eisenstein went on to say. "Everything you do that comes from love . . . is a prayer, a message to the living earth: You are not alone."

The frequency of forest fires where I live in southern Oregon has increased dramatically over the last decade. So last summer, when we had a long, dry heat wave followed by gathering thunder clouds, emergency officials sent out texts to prepare the public for the possibility of multiple fires caused by lightning strikes. The skies darkened. Lightning flashed across the valley. Social media lit up with laments from neighbors anticipating the coming fire and smoke.

But then, unexpectedly, the storms were followed by rain—great heaps of rain that poured across our region all night and into the early morning. By daybreak the various lightning fires had been doused. The sun sparkled in a clear blue sky.

When I stepped out of the house that morning, I could smell the rainwater. Everything felt fresh and green and especially vibrant. And there, in the branches of our walnut tree, I spotted a scrub jay. Curious and alive, hopping from limb to limb.

11

SACRED STORIES

My friend Riley sent me a news story from a newspaper in Reykjavik, Iceland, entitled, "Missing Woman Unknowingly Joins Search for Herself." A woman visiting Iceland joined a bus tour to a national volcanic park. During one stop, the woman went into a building and changed her clothes. When she returned to the bus, none of her traveling companions recognized her, so they reported her missing. When the depiction of the "missing" woman was circulated, the woman who had changed her outfit didn't recognize the description of herself. So she joined the search party.

For two days the missing woman worked with a group of fifty people to scan the surrounding area and distribute leaflets with a depiction of herself. The article states: "Eventually it occurred to the 'missing' woman that she could very well be the person everyone was looking for. She promptly reported herself safe and sound to the police."

In this culture it is so easy to suffer amnesia. Life today is like living inside a giant warehouse store—most days we find ourselves wandering aimlessly through fluorescent aisles eating samples of kale chips, comparing prices on cat climbers despite not owning a cat. We are forgetting creatures, and the bustling world preys on our forgetting.

The hard work of life is remembering. Remembering who you are, remembering how you want to be in the world, remembering where you last left the kids. Down through the centuries our ancestors have told and retold stories to help us find our way. Sacred stories that remind us of our true identity. Soul stories to encourage us to pursue our deepest yearnings for freedom. Told from one seeking heart to another, these sacred stories function like a lighthouse— guiding us away from the shallows, leading us toward the more gracious depths of who we are.

When asked why he spoke in parables, Jesus told his followers (as paraphrased by Anthony de Mello): The shortest distance between truth and a human being is a story. All wisdom traditions entrust stories to embody their deepest truths. The Bible is full of stories. The Bhagavad Gita is a story. The Buddha's life teachings are embedded in story form. The life of Muhammad is transmitted through story. Jesus's life and teachings are communicated through story.

Science is also a story that seeks to unveil reality and dispel illusion. Behind the doctrine, the rules, the rituals, and the institutions of all wisdom traditions, you find stories that not only seek to transmit teachings but invite a deeper, more liberating experience of the self and the world.

The power of stories to free us, whether religious or secular, depends on the integrity and compassion of the tellers and the openness of the listeners. The sacred stories of religion are often at first glance amusing relics, utter nonsense, even potentially destructive—unless they are shared by people who are knowledgeable and trustworthy. Only within the sacred bond of compassionate teller and seeking listener can we know a story's worth. It is within that trusting container where we can give ourselves to the story. There we can expose our hurt and longing to its plotlines and allow the story to read us. There we can allow ourselves to enter the story. Not as fact. More than fact. As a way of seeing, as a gateway to peace, as a pathway home.

There we can allow ourselves to fall into the story's rhythms and feel its truths. The same way we might give our body to the steps of a dance in order to feel its joy. Slow, slow, quick-quick, slow, quick-quick, slow, slow.

———

I was in a lost, longing-for-meaning place in my midtwenties. For about six months I could hardly sleep more than a handful of hours. All the repressed wounds of my childhood were radiating out from me like a high-grade fever. There was a terrifying emptiness gathering within me, a gnawing sense of worthlessness, and the only way I knew to address it was to stay busy and distract myself from the anxiety by working and working and working. I became mindlessly driven, physically ragged, deeply sleep deprived. My marriage suffered and my health deteriorated. I began to obsess about finding a new job, certain that different employment would give me some sense of peace.

It took a good friend and colleague to recognize my crisis was more than vocational. Tenderly, persistently, he convinced me to join him on a contemplative retreat at a Franciscan convent. I agreed—but only under the ridiculous stipulation that I could commute home each night to catch up on work.

There are parts of ourselves that can't be known, places within us that can't be accessed without a story. The week at the Franciscan convent was destabilizing. Full of silence, prayer, long periods of solitude, I was forced to feel the stark, despairing state I was in. I was lost and hurting and had no idea what to do. Every morning the retreat teacher gave a talk and then offered a spiritual practice. Each talk was based on a story that sought to uncover our deeper nature.

One morning he told us the story of the prodigal son, one of the parables of Jesus.

A man has two sons. The younger son is restless, impatient. He goes to his father and asks for his half of the inheritance. The father agrees. The son takes the money, heads into the nearby city, and eventually spends it all on parties, prostitutes, dissolute living. A famine descends upon the land. Broke, desperate, working for a pig farmer to feed himself, the young man decides to return home, apologize, and see if he might be hired as a farmhand—a much better life than his current state. While walking the road home, the father sees his son and takes off running. Before the

younger son can fully apologize, the father embraces him, places
his rings on his son's fingers, and instructs the servants to prepare
a celebration.

Meanwhile the elder son is out working in the fields. He hears
music and revelry. He asks one of the field hands to investigate.
"Your brother has returned," the field hand reports. "Your father
is throwing a celebration." The elder brother is greatly triggered
by this news. Filled with resentment, he refuses to join the party.
The father hears the response of his eldest. He leaves the festiv-
ities, goes out into the fields, and begs his son to join the party.
The elder son is indignant. He reminds his father of his loyalty,
frugality, and hard work. How could he celebrate a son who has
been so self-serving, disrespectful, and wasteful? The father feels
compassion for his eldest boy. He reminds him everything else he
has belongs to his eldest. The father adds, "But we had to rejoice
because this brother of yours was dead and has come to life, was .
blind but now he sees."

The retreat teacher invited us to personally interact
with the parable. We were sent out to find a solitary place
to meditate on the story, with instructions to try and see,
hear, taste, smell, and feel the story as if we were there. He
encouraged us to go wherever the meditation took us—allow
ourselves to become one of the characters, place the story
in a modern setting, or change the characters from a father
and two sons to a mother and two daughters if helpful.

I found an empty basement classroom in the convent,
sat alone in the dark, and as instructed, gave my imagination over to the story of the prodigal son. I saw the dust of

the road, heard the goats and sheep in the nearby field. I saw the sons, the eldest responsibly and dutifully heading out to the fields, the younger son pacing, dissatisfied. As if it were an old home movie, I watched the story take place within me.

I have no idea how much time passed, but then something happened. Like a lucid dream, I fell into the story. I could smell the dry earth, feel the sun on my back, hear the distant laughter and music from a party. I was the elder brother. I felt depleted, isolated, hopeless, full of resentment—and then surprisingly, in the midst of this story-dreaming, I felt a visceral sense of overwhelming welcome, a sense of being held. An unburdening, a release, a compassionate embrace. I wept, and the aloneness and fear and sense of failure I had been carrying dissipated.

When I finally pulled myself together, I immediately wondered if I was having some kind of psychological breakdown. The experience was so powerful I thought I might be losing my mind. I went to find the retreat leader, Morton Kelsey, who was not only an Episcopal priest but also a trained psychotherapist of forty years. I assumed he would offer a diagnosis and recommend medication or therapy or possibly even some time in an institution.

Troubled and disoriented, I found Morton in the cafeteria and asked if he would meet with me. After evening prayer we found a quiet place to talk. I told him my experience of the meditation, fully expecting him to become alarmed. Instead he told me a story, one about growing up with a father who could be quite remote and demanding. He then asked me about my own upbringing, my relationship with my parents. I answered as best I could.

Then he told me a story about his first job. Back and forth we went, like village bells answering one another across a valley, with various experiences from our lives. Whatever note I struck in my story, he would strike a similar note, allowing me to feel heard and understood. For almost three hours we sat facing one another, telling stories, back and forth, back and forth, until there was a deeply felt connection. Eventually the hour became late, our words spent. Morton stood to leave, and I suddenly realized he had not answered my question.

"But what about the meditation? Was it a breakdown?"

"Well," he said thoughtfully. "What do you think? We've been talking for hours. You seem calm. You're speaking coherently. Your body seems relaxed. You don't seem agitated in any way. It doesn't appear to me you are having a psychotic break. Maybe it was something else? Maybe it was Divine Love. Maybe it was God."

———

"There must always be two kinds of art," writes poet W. H. Auden. "Escape art, for humans need escape as we need food and deep sleep, and parable art, the art which shall teach us to unlearn hatred and learn love." My experience at the Franciscan convent is the sacred story of how I began to live from a deeper awareness of love and truth. It was the beginning of a healing season for me that included therapy, long talks with my wife, a commitment to spiritual practice, a different approach to work.

My friends who are secular humanists would tell it another way. They might describe my experience as a breakthrough of the unconscious or of transference of care from teacher to student. I'm okay with that. But since it is my sacred story, I tell it in the way that feels most true for me.

Your sacred story may have a different setting. Maybe it takes place at a bowling alley, a community center, a mountain lake, a grandmother's kitchen, a desert plateau, a detention center, a Girl Scout camp. Maybe your story begins in divorce, the wake of grief, the ecstasy of nature, a quest for truth, a near-death experience, a restless longing for love. And in your story you might replace the Episcopal priest with a molecular biologist, a Holocaust survivor, a cognitive therapist, a Buddhist nun, a Native American elder, the old guy who lived next door. And in your story, instead of a Jesus parable, there might be a conversation about galaxies, a pilgrimage to your mother's home village, a letter from a trusted friend, a mindfulness practice, a month of solitude in a Minnesota cabin, a heartfelt conversation with your best friend's father, a stranger's confession in an AA group.

There is a depth to story that we rarely take time to ponder, let alone to tell and hear. Story is how we transform pain. Story is how we make something useful out of the absurd. A sacred story is a love letter expanding your heart with kindness. A sacred story is a treasure box filled with images of what matters most. A sacred story is a map, passed down through generations, directing you toward a fountain of truth. A sacred story is a medicine, a balm to relieve your fear and suffering. A sacred story is an angel in the night. A sacred story is a window that offers perspective. Sometimes a sacred story is a shield, a protector, a source of courage and love. Sometimes your sacred story is what gives you strength to face the real and present dangers of our world. Sometimes your sacred story spends years searching for you, trailing you through all your harried days, cornering you in some blue fluorescent rehab center, looking you in the eye, and saying, "Okay, here's the truth."

What are the images, the moments, the stories on which your soul meditates? What are the stories that remind you to unlearn hatred and receive love? Nigerian author Ben Okri declared, "We live by stories. We also live in them. One way or another, we are living the stories planted in us early or along the way, or we are also living the stories we planted—knowingly or unknowingly—in ourselves. We live stories that either give our lives meaning or negate it with meaninglessness. If we change the stories we live by, quite possibly, we change our lives."

Are the stories that shape you death dealing or life giving? Do the stories you hold as sacred heal, or do they exacerbate the suffering? Do they bring out your loving nature, do they cultivate freedom? Or do they bum you out, make you more afraid, anxious, resentful, and bitter? What are the stories you hold as sacred, the ones you tell your children, the ones you want remembered at your funeral? And are they any good?

———

It's perilous to have no story to live by, to live unmoored, vulnerable to the currents of the surrounding culture. This may be a great source of anxiety and depression today: no sacred story to help us make sense in a senseless world. Each of us needs a story to anchor our lives. We look to the great texts, novels, sacred scrolls, and hope to find a story that will give us some kind of direction for shaping our lives. In the right setting and transmitted with care, these stories can transform us. Yet sometimes the story we need most waits patiently within us.

When leading retreats and workshops, I often start with an exercise that seeks to draw out these sacred stories. I invite participants to recall a moment in their lives that they would name as sacred. The moment doesn't need to be particularly life changing or spiritual in any way. In fact, it might be a moment that is quite ordinary. I ask them to imagine being given a photo album that contains a picture from every moment of their lives. I invite them to use their imagination to travel back in time and relive whatever memory comes to them, recalling the sensory details—what they saw, heard, touched, and felt. After about ten minutes of silently ruminating within their particular memory, people gather in small groups to share their experience. One by one they tell their sacred story:

> *I remembered the first morning I dropped my daughter off at school . . .*
> *I was fourteen, looking at this prehistoric handprint . . .*
> *My grandfather had just died and my mother was crying . . .*
> *There were four of us walking the Pacific Crest Trail, and we came to this lookout . . .*
> *I stood barefoot in the snow after my first week sober . . .*

Carl Jung once wrote that the soul speaks in images. Within our small retreat groups, each person spools out the sacred images that came to them in the meditation. The listeners silently bear witness, responding at times with nods, smiles, eyes glistening with tears. And after each soul has had its say, for a brief moment, we feel ourselves held. Carried by something that can never quite be named.

———

In an older world it was understood that you had to go in search of wisdom. You couldn't Google it. You had to ask around. Look for the one guy who could read. Stalk the hermit lady back to her cabin. Keep knocking even when she threatened to turn you into a newt. For most of human history, truth was sparse and wisdom rare. When it came to finding meaning, suffering could be quite useful. You needed some hard luck, some failure, a painful loss to drive you to sell your possessions, find a pilgrim stick, and head down the road searching for . . . what? You weren't sure. A place? Maybe a person? Someone who knew what the hell it's all about. Someone who could speak the question you didn't know how to ask.

Grubby, lonely, and ready to give up, you would come across an enlightened woodsman, a beekeeping anchorite, a praying imam, an itinerant monk, an Episcopal priest, a particularly thoughtful frog. Seeing your distress, they'd offer you drink, a little food, a place to rest. And then the kind figure would address your existential suffering with a story. A story designed to transfigure you. A story packed with spiritual nutrients. A story that offered meaning without defining it. A story that held up a more generous identity than you had been willing to hold of yourself. And your interior emptiness, your soul like a starved baby bird—crying, mouth open—would listen carefully, meditate on it, until over time, the truth of the story could finally be swallowed, digested, embodied.

INTERLUDE

THE FAUN

Not long after our daughter turned three, she refused to wear most items of clothing. Every article felt wrong—too bumpy, too tight, too scratchy, too twisty. Unable to take our barely clad daughter to the library, grocery store, play dates, or basically any outing, we became housebound, especially in the cold of winter.

Weeks into Gracie's minimalist stage, we were desperate to get out of the house. I walked into her room armed with candy, stuffed animals, and chocolate milk. None of it worked.

"Too loose! Too loose!" she called out and threw her clothes to the floor. Immediately I began telling a story to distract her. "Gracie! Did you know there's a faun who lives in the woods above our street named Tooloose? If you keep yelling his name, he may even come to the window!"

Gracie ran to the window. "Where?" I pointed to the mountains. "Up there. He lives up there in the faun village." I launched into a story about Tooloose, the fauns, and a trusted girl named Gracie.

"That's my name!"

"What a strange coincidence . . ."

Slowly, gingerly, I surreptitiously dressed her while talking animatedly about the fauns from the mountains. As long as the story continued, she listened and—best of all—kept her clothes on.

After that winter evening, I continued to tell stories of Tooloose the Faun and his many adventures with Gracie. Months went by, and her clothing issues eventually ceased. The stories had become so compelling that Gracie asked me to take her up into the mountains to see if we could find this legendary faun village and the impish Tooloose.

One afternoon we drove up into the woods and hiked among the trails. At the top of one ridge, we found a cluster of enormous granite boulders, ten to twenty feet tall, rounded with soft mats of lichen. We sat among these boulders and I told Gracie a story of how the fauns disguised their homes to look like boulders so they could remain hidden from human beings. Gracie was excited by this description and began foraging among the boulders looking for signs of faun life. Before long she spotted an old campfire—surely a faun campfire—scattered with rusting cans of Pabst Blue Ribbon. Gracie hoisted a beer can above her head, "This is what the fauns drink!" Over the next hour we found tree bark (faun paper), smooth branches (used in faun stick games), and an XL pair of men's underwear (for large-bottomed fauns).

From that day on, Gracie asked me to take her on regular faun hunts. She no longer wanted to find faun artifacts; she wanted to meet the fauns for real. Many afternoons, we went hiking in the woods or searching along the trails above our city park, looking for fauns. Some days Gracie would leave notes promising the fauns we were friendly and meant no harm. Other days she left handfuls of flowers, a drawing of her and the fauns holding hands, or walnut shells filled with tiny candies. Gracie would leave these gifts and then ask me to address the fauns hiding in the woods. "Fauns!" I would call into the empty trees, "Fauns, we are friends! I am here with my daughter Gracie, and she is very kind and loving and she promises not tell anyone where you live. Please, fauns, don't be afraid. Come out and see us."

Then we would wait and wait for the fauns that never appeared. One day Gracie fell to the ground and asked me with such sadness, "Why don't they come out, Dad?"

I suddenly feared that I had pushed her imagination too far. "Gracie," I began, "Maybe the fauns just live in stories—"

"Don't say that, Dad. Don't say they only live in stories. Fauns are real. I know it." I remained silent, not sure how to negotiate her feelings.

For at least a year, Gracie and I returned to the woods to look for fauns. Each time, Gracie insisted on leaving gifts or notes and calling for them to come out of hiding. They never showed. I began to get a sick feeling that my stories were causing real harm. I knew that in Gracie's mind, the fauns remained in hiding because they didn't know if they could trust her. Each time they didn't show, Gracie felt it was a reflection on her character.

After many trips into the mountains, Gracie wondered if I might be the problem. "Dad, let's look for fauns one more time. But Dad, I can tell you are pretending to look for them. You have to *really* look for them. You have to believe in them. Okay?"

"All right," I said.

"Promise?"

"Promise."

And I tried, as best I could, to really look for fauns. I called out, I crawled under bushes and looked behind trees. Nothing. And then Gracie asked me to hoist her onto one of the boulders. I shouldered her up and there she stood, closing her eyes and singing the most precious song to the fauns, promising them she was kind and good and that they could come out and she would be their true, true friend.

My heart sank. I had ruined my perfectly trusting daughter with lies about fauns. Her song ended, we stood in the silence, and I felt Gracie's heart break. I tried to comfort her, but she did not want to hear my adult excuses. She knew the fauns, she knew they only appeared to those who were trustworthy. She must not be trustworthy.

As we walked down the mountain and back into the city park, we began to hear the lilting sounds of a flute. We stepped out from behind some rhododendron bushes and followed the melody out onto a grass clearing.

And there, playing a carved wooden flute, was a faun.

A faun with furry legs, a bare chest, and two horns protruding from the top of his head. A faun with long, tangled, muddy hair, a goatee, and an eye mask made of green oak leaves. A faun playing music while dancing a little jig.

Gracie and I were dumbstruck.

The faun was actually just a guy. Some strange shirtless guy, dressed in fur pants with deer antlers wired to his head and a home-made mask of oak leaves rubber-banded to his face. Gracie was mesmerized. I was slightly alarmed.

The faun guy stopped playing his flute and smiled at us. Still holding my hand, Gracie whispered, "Talk to him." I realized I had no choice but to play this out.

We approached the faun. "My name is Mark and this is my daughter, Gracie. We have been looking for you for months. We have left gifts for you and notes for you, and we are so glad to have finally found you."

"I'm glad you found me, too!" the young antlered man said with a smile. I turned to Gracie and whispered, "Do you want to say anything?" She shook her head no. I told him again how grateful we were to see him and that we meant him no harm and that Gracie always trusted that he existed and she was a good person and would never do anything to harm him or his faun relatives.

"I can see that you are a good person," he said to Gracie. "Take care of the forest, treat it with care, and any time you want to see me, just come up this trail and look over into those bushes where I often sleep." I looked over and spotted what appeared to be a back-pack and sleeping bag.

The faun bowed, and Gracie and I took off running down the hill and into the park. We ran laughing and hollering, "We saw a faun! We saw a faun! We saw a faun!" When we came to the bottom of the trail, Gracie danced. "I knew it, I knew it!" she shouted. "You see, Dad? Now do you believe?"

12

HOME

A local nonprofit committed to humanistic ideals decided to hold a retreat to help their membership reconnect to their mission statement: "Promoting critical thinking and freedom from religion and superstition." The problem was none of them had ever been on a retreat. So they called and asked if I would be willing to design and facilitate the gathering. I confessed to them that although I shared a number of their values, I was not a secular humanist myself, and in fact was someone whose beliefs they would probably consider suspect. The leadership said they would overlook this particular shortcoming as long as I was willing to refrain from any crazy God talk.

I crafted a schedule and was asked to present it to the board. At various points in the retreat, I had planned moments for people to share stories in small groups to get at the core vitality and values of the organization—stories about why they joined the secular humanist group, stories about life-giving experiences within the club, and the like.

A board member listened to my presentation and then questioned all the scheduled storytelling.

"This isn't group therapy," she told me.

"How can we find the heart of this group without inviting people to share stories?" I responded.

"By looking at the facts," she answered.

The next day, I had coffee with one of our local rabbis—a rabbi who had been raised by secular Jewish parents, a rabbi who had hitchhiked across America as a young man on a spiritual quest. A rabbi who once told a funny story at The Hearth about a fistfight he had in high school with a tough classmate called "Cheeser." Rabbi Joshua listened carefully to my struggle to create a visioning retreat for the secular humanists. When I told him they were strongly against religion, he replied, "Yes, I understand. But how can you live without stories?"

Our world is in crisis. It's clear the stories we've been telling ourselves as a civilization are killing us. Fear is wisdom. Greed is responsible. Vanity is virtuous. Violence is peacemaking. Martin Luther King Jr. believed that the destructive stories and myths at the root of white American culture come from a moral illness, a soul sickness. In the face of these damaging stories, the secular humanists make a good point: Facts are essential. Facts tell us the earth is heating up. Facts point out systemic violence and racial injustice. Facts help surgeons locate and remove the cancer. We need facts.

But facts can't hold us together. Facts can't inspire us beyond our present sufferings. Facts can't answer the deep cry within us for meaning. Not unless you line them up in a story first.

We need scientists, journalists, truth-tellers who seek to accurately chart the longitude and latitude of our living. But we can't become fully human without the cartographers of the soul. Artists, dream-weavers, visionaries, storytellers who coax our spirits to love and create and inhabit a more generous world. Oscar Wilde once said, "A map without utopia on it is not even worth glancing at." The question is: Who will tell the story? Where do we find the dreams and visions we need at this time in our history? If the old stories can't be trusted, where do the new stories come from?

In the United States, there is a real poverty when it comes to narrating a world worth striving for. Our collective imagination is stunted. Maybe it's because we've been betrayed too many times, suffered false promises, watched as leaders and trusted institutions manipulated our deepest longings. Maybe we've grown cynical.

Or maybe we haven't yet storied our way into a more loving and compelling future because we've never reckoned with our past. We continually resist acknowledging the slavery, genocide, racism, misogyny, environmental destruction, and other atrocities intimately woven throughout our history. Many of us cling to the old stories because we don't want to lose the privileges and exalted identities that those biased histories provide us. Whatever the cause, it is clear we have few visions, few common stories that describe the world we all long to live in. The upheaval of this present time provides an opportunity to tell a new story. But that new story cannot bring healing and hope until those who have been silenced finally have the platform to be heard.

Civil rights activist and Harvard lecturer Marshall Ganz claims that story is about "how people make choices when they are confronted with not knowing what to do." Maybe we are in the messy middle of the story. The crux. The dark unknown. Maybe we are at the end of the first act, that moment when the real struggle is brought forth. Maybe we are at that turning point where the only way forward is together.

Indian writer and political activist Arundhati Roy captures the way in which the coronavirus pandemic has lifted up the choice humanity faces in crafting a new story: "What is this thing that has happened to us? It has brought the world to a halt like nothing else could. It offers us a chance to rethink the doomsday machine we have built for ourselves. Nothing could be worse than a return to normality. Historically, pandemics have forced human beings to break with the past and imagine their world anew. This one is no different. It is a portal, a gateway between one world and the next. We can choose to walk through it, dragging the carcasses of our prejudice and hatred, our avarice, our data banks and dead ideas, our dead rivers and smoky skies behind us. Or we can walk through lightly, with little luggage, ready to imagine another world. And ready to fight for it."

In the spring of 2019, The Hearth launched a training model to explore the use of storytelling to heal, enrich, and mobilize communities for good. Fifty-five teachers, activists, artists, nonprofit leaders, mediators, pastors, and other community-builders signed up. They came from Denver, Oakland, Baton Rouge, Seattle, Anchorage, Austin, Portland, Chicago, and towns across the Pacific Northwest. Together we explored how stories function in our personal and public lives. We practiced the skills of deep listening and telling. We discerned how stories imprison or liberate. We graphed our stories in order to understand their shapes and movements. We diagrammed joy. Plotted the rise and fall of tragedy. Outlined the backward loop of redemption and the upward swing of courage. We talked about the conditions needed to make the power of storytelling accessible and available to communities. We tried out various story methods, struggled to make conscious the conditions that invite human honesty and vulnerability, noted the rare gift of a good question. And then everyone went back to their communities and started experimenting.

Seven months later the group reconvened and shared what they had done. Lily Kaplan explained how she set up a "story tent" at an Overdose Awareness Day in Southern Oregon. The white canvas tent had tables, writing materials, a clothesline with signs inviting people to share stories about their loved ones. Lily and her friends knew that when a person dies from an opioid addiction, their family and friends are often left fixated on their loved one's addiction and death. The story tent was designed to help survivors recollect the life-giving attributes and characteristics of the people who had died in order to bring some healing and peace. One by one people entered the tent and wrote down remembrances of their loved ones according to the prompts: a memory that makes you smile or laugh, an adventure you shared, a time when you experienced the gifts of your loved one. Stories were written, displayed, and read out loud at the gathering.

Robbie Goldman, who works with an agency serving homeless youth in downtown Denver, gathered volunteers to help create a pop-up museum at the Denver Rockies' Memorial Hall at Coors Stadium. The museum held sacred objects from various youth who live on the streets: a Houston Rockets T-shirt, a dog collar, a blue comb, a Denny's menu. All the collected items were set out with stories written by the young people explaining the meaning behind their particular objects. Goldman invited the public to visit the museum and pay attention to how these familiar objects and accompanying stories revealed our common humanity.

Alessandra de la Torres realized the activists and marginalized people who attend her "Know Your Rights Training" needed a stronger sense of self to actually employ their civil rights when confronted by police. Rather than simply providing information, she had participants begin the workshop by sitting in small groups and sharing stories based on a moment they stood up for someone, a time someone stood up for them, and an encounter in which they felt valued by another person. After each story-sharing, she had people notice the emotions present in these stories and the sense of self experienced in the listening and telling. Then she had participants take physical postures that expressed the dignity and worth they felt in their stories in order to help them access and embody the strength required to fully claim their rights.

Shannon Savage-Howe shared how she trained a team of volunteers to record written and oral stories from the people of Thousand Oaks, California, in the aftermath of a mass shooting and two devastating wildfires suffered within the same week. Journalist Phil Manzano shared videos from a storytelling campaign he helped orchestrate in south Seattle to highlight the rich cultural diversity of local business owners and community leaders in a time of rapid gentrification. Community organizer Michelle Glass described how she used story circles to help a small town build the relationships and courage needed to prevent a neo-Nazi group that was starting to organize a local Neighborhood Watch. One by one the participants described how they helped repair broken families, cultivate empathy within bitter city government meetings, revive relationships among depleted hospital staff members, and draw out honest conversation within racially divided neighborhoods. They did this by going back to the basics of human interaction—gathering people together to share what they had lived, loved, suffered, and overcome.

If humanity is to survive and flourish, we need to do the slow work of congregating and exchanging stories and lessons from what we have lived. We need to nurture our capacities to listen well and speak honestly. If we are to recover the angels of our better nature, we have to move at soul speeds. We can't simply replace the old stories with the new. We have to pay attention to who is talking and who is listening. We have to notice who is there and who is missing. We have to go out and coax those who have been excluded from the conversation to share what they know to be true.

Buddhist teacher Pema Chödrön has a practice she often uses when encountering other people. Quietly within herself she simply says, *just like me*. The person may be sad or angry, acting with kindness or behaving badly—elbowing people through an airport, speaking harshly to a child, hoarding pie at the community potluck. *Just like me*, Pema says to herself. *They are just like me.* We are much more similar than the political and media storytellers would have us believe. For these similarities to be felt and known, we have to spend more time with one another. We need to uncover the stories that reveal our connectedness. We need to gather when the crisis hits. We need to allow suffering to speak. We need to move closer to one another, preferably within earshot, when we sense the anxiety, hurt, and fear rising.

We need to feel the warmth of one another if we are to work up any trust, if we are to discover the new stories, if we are to create a larger, more beautiful vision of the world.

———

During the six months I lived and worked in Austin, Texas, I hoped to create a series of public story events to highlight the passions and concerns of twenty-somethings. Before I did this work, I wanted to visit the grassroots story groups that already existed.

I was surprised at how many I found: Testify, Backyard Story Night, Tales from Queer Mountain, Story Bar, Bed-Post Confessions, Moon Language Story Circle, Beyond Our Backyard, Story X, Truth Fact Fiction, Mortified, The Living Room. Some of these gatherings were formal, others informal. Some focused on the craft of story, others on the community and compassion that stories create. Despite their differences, each story group was made up of young adults longing for human connection. At each gathering I felt these young people trying to birth themselves out of the ruins of consumer culture and failed religion.

One June night, I attended a group called Moon Language Story Circle, which met at an urban farm each month during a full moon. This particular June gathering was being held at Aqua Dulce Farm on the outskirts of Austin. Cars were parked along a dirt road, and people wandered through rows of greenhouses to get to a grass field behind the farmhouse. A few tables were set out for the potluck food and drink. The mostly millennial crowd filled plates and then sat in the grass, visiting as dusk alighted the sky. After an hour or so, Josh Blaine, the convener for the evening, asked "anyone with a story, a song, a poem, or a ritual" to meet by the barn. I walked over and gathered in the circle with others. Josh instructed each of us to share our name and summarize our offering: An astronomical reading of the stars. A poem. A ukulele duet. A story about a midnight bike ride. And so on. Josh listened and then created the order for the evening, "Let's have you explain the night sky to start, then how about the poem followed by your song, and then the stories. . . ." Once we all knew our places, we returned to the group. The moon was full and people carried blankets and camping chairs as they gathered around a crackling fire.

Josh welcomed the group, and immediately someone raised a hand to announce they had brought a bottle of homemade mead. They invited everyone to drink from it as a symbol of our shared humanity. People applauded. The big bottle was passed around. A young woman then stood and asked us to gaze at the night stars. She pointed out the various constellations and explained the movement of the planets, particularly the positioning of Saturn and its meaning in the ancient world. We were quiet, eyes gazing, chins tilted upward. The woman sat, and a young bearded man read a poem from his journal about his failed search for self. Then two women took out ukuleles and sang a song they'd written called "Lake of Stars." Another poem was recited. And then the stories were shared, each teller walking around the fire as they told their tale.

An hour or so passed. "Anyone else have a story to share?" Josh asked. When the group remained silent, a man in rough work clothes stood. "I spent today cutting brush, and there was this really fragrant rosemary. Seemed like a waste to throw in the yard trucks, so I brought it here." He began handing out branches of rosemary to each of us. "I thought maybe we could each say something we want to let go of, and then throw our branches into the fire."

The young man sat. A silence descended, and then one by one people stood by the fire and spoke.

"I want to let go of my insecurity."

"I want to let go of my bitterness."

"I want to let go of my debilitating fear of the future."

"I want to let go of my dad."

The flames rose up, billows of white smoke shifted according to the breeze, the camphor scent of rosemary surrounded us.

The ritual ended, and Josh took out a guitar and invited people to sing. It was an old spiritual, "Will the Circle be Unbroken." No one really knew the song, so Josh called out each line before it was sung. It is a kind of lament that begins with the singer standing at a window watching a hearse pass by, carrying the body of the singer's mother. The singer begs the undertaker to drive slowly, to delay the separation of death. The words and images expressed that primal human longing for relationship, for connection, to be eternally held within a family of human beings even in the midst of loss.

The language of the hymn was from another time and place, but those gathered felt the emotion and sang it out, allowing their own mixed and dormant yearnings to rise to the surface:

Will the circle be unbroken
By and by, by and by?
Is a better home a-waiting
In the sky, in the sky?

The facts of this world will never satisfy the human heart. We need a destination. We ache for the promise of being welcomed and received by those we love. We long for a homecoming. "If we didn't believe in homecoming we couldn't bear the day," poet W. S. Merwin once stated. It is that belief, that yearning, that drives our most treasured stories.

My father died after a car accident on a rural freeway off-ramp, by himself, twenty miles from his home. In the last hours of his life, we as his family were given many facts—the particulars of the accident, the nature of his injuries, the medical interventions that were attempted and failed. Then he died, and we were left helpless in the face of that ultimate fact, which is beyond the heart's comprehension.

Two weeks after my father's death, my family received a handwritten letter from members of the Hornbrook Fire Department. In the letter they shared their experience of the accident—the initial call from emergency services, the rush to respond, what they found when they arrived on the scene. They recounted that my father was found unconscious, yet they described how they spoke to him with words of comfort and encouragement. They reported how they tended his wounds and how, when the moment came to lift and carry his body to the emergency vehicle, they acted with gentleness, respect, and love. They closed the letter by expressing their condolences and their hope that, by sharing their story, they could offer the family some comfort and peace. The letter was signed, simply, the Hornbrook Fire Department.

I have never met the members of the Hornbrook Fire Department. I do not know the names of the people who cared for my father in his last hours. What I do know is that I needed to hear their story. What I know is that through their story, their hands became my hands, their words my words.

Every act of love brings hope. Every act of love ushers the new world into the present. Every act of love bridges alienation, brings comfort to our fears, makes space for hope. We need stories to help us recall the things we've all forgotten: That we are intimately interrelated. That our home is in one another. That peace is found within one another.

We live in a world that is alive and generous and in need of care. Strangely, paradoxically, it is in serving and singing and telling our stories to one another that we discover the homecoming we've been longing for has been here, among and within us, all along.

ACKNOWLEDGMENTS

First and last gratitudes, all earthly possessions, unending love forever and ever amen to my wife and bestest friend, Jill. This book took countless rewrites, reconceptions, and edits over three years and represents over ten years in community storytelling work. Through it all, Jill has been a faithful workmate, compassionate listener, sharp editor, and loving companion. If not for her humble objection, she would be credited as coauthor.

Annie Lamott has been a kind, brilliant, and steadfast champion of this book, my work, and me. Her careful reading, exuberant praise ("I swear on my dog Ladybird this is the best chapter!") and ruthless edits ("Was this paragraph written by you or the Democratic National Committee?" and "Just waking up after napping through last three pages . . . did I miss anything?") saved readers a lot of unnecessary slogging.

Heartfelt thanks to my good buddy Duane Whitcomb who spent many walks and late-night IPAs patiently listening, empathizing, and providing wise counsel as I developed The Hearth and grew in my understanding of community storytelling.

Founding board members Mark DiRienzo and Ben Bellinson are the guys you want by your side when embarking on any journey. Their loyal friendship, competent advice, and generosity have been a consistent source of support and encouragement.

Thanks to my dear friend Melissa Wiginton, who provided a number of teaching opportunities at Austin Presbyterian Theological Seminary where I put together the original ideas that became the roots of this book.

Big love to my friend and fellow Oregonian Max Gimbel. Max was one of the first persons to see the potential of storytelling as a community building practice. His friendship, humor, and trust has been life altering.

Thanks to my oldest pal Kirk Wulf for a phone call in 2009 in which he said, "You should work with story."

Sincere thanks to agent Kimberley Cameron for securing a safe harbor for this book, to Valerie Weaver-Zercher for her careful editing and enthusiasm, and to the staff at Broadleaf for their care and belief in this work.

I have been given heaps of joy and made a better person by my three hilarious, soulful, gifted, and loving children: Noah, Joseph, and Gracie. Love you three wonderful nerds.

Finally, this book would not be possible without the many people, organizations, and communities who have trusted me with their stories. Because of you I have become more alive, more compassionate, more whole. Thank you from the bottom of my heart.

For more information on The Hearth and community storytelling trainings go to www.thehearthcommunity.com.

NOTES

Chapter 1

7   *"All sorrows can be borne"*: Isak Dinesen, as cited by Jack Maquire, *The Power of Personal Storytelling: Spinning Tales to Connect with Others* (New York: Jeremy P. Tarcher/Putnam, 1998), 17.

9   *"a wordless story"*: Resmaa Menakem, *My Grandmother's Hands* (Las Vegas, NV: Central Recovery Press, 2017), 5.

Chapter 2

18   *"There is no greater agony"*: Maya Angelou, *Rainbow in the Cloud: The Wisdom and Spirit of Maya Angelou* (New York: Random House, 2014), 51.

Chapter 3

43   *"what you wanted"*: Tristine Rainer, *Your Life as Story: Writing the New Autobiography* (New York: G. P. Putnam's Sons, 1997), 38.

Chapter 4

50   *"as enemy, fright, other"*: Adrienne Maree Brown, *Emergent Strategy: Shaping Change, Changing Worlds* (Chico, CA: AK Press, 2017), 21.

52   *"In order to hear family stories"*: Rebecca Solnit, interview by Tess Thackara, White Review, June 23, 2013.

52   *"intergenerational self"*: Marshall Duke, "The Stories That Bind Us: What Are the Twenty Questions?," *HuffPost* (blog), March 23, 2013.

Chapter 5

60   *"Over half a million marketers"*: Michael de Groot, "Do You Call Yourself a Storyteller?" Medium, July 17, 2018, www.medium.com/typewriting. According to de Groot over 550,000 marketers label themselves "storytellers" within their LinkedIn profile.

61   *"When you watch them"*: Adam Alter, "'Irresistible' by Design: It's No Accident You Can't Stop Looking at the Screen," interview by Terri Gross, *Fresh Air*, March 13, 2017.

Chapter 6

78   *"An authentic story is about us"*: Sacred Land Film Project, "Barry Lopez on Storytelling," YouTube, August 28, 2017, www.youtube.com.

84   *"We are separate"*: TEDx Talks, "A New Story of the People: Charles Eisenstein at TEDx Whitechapel," YouTube, February 13, 2013, https://www.youtube.com/watch?v=Mjoxh4c2Dj0.

85   *"Listening is an act"*: U. K. Le Guin, *Words Are My Matter: Writings on Life and Books* (Boston: HMH Books, 2019), 6.

85   *"More picnics"*: *10 Questions for the Dalai Lama* (Monterrey Media, 2006), DVD.

87   *"blowing on the embers"*: Elizabeth Ellis, cited by Jack Maquire, *The Power of Personal Storytelling: Spinning Tales to Connect with Others* (New York: Jeremy P. Tarcher/Putnam, 1998), 208.

Chapter 7

99   *"Who is this"*: Mary Oliver, *Winter Hours: Prose, Prose Poems, and Poems* (Boston: Houghton Mifflin Company, 2000), 33.

Chapter 9

123   *"Horrible in itself"*: Rebecca Solnit, *Paradise in Hell: The Extraordinary Communities That Arise in Disaster* (New York: Penguin, 2009), 3.

Chapter 10

137   *"is the worst thing"*: Thich Nhat Hanh, *At Home in the World* (Berkeley: Parallax Press, 2016), 48.

137   *"Will you revert"*: John Yorke, *Into the Woods: A Five-Act Journey into Story* (New York: Overlook Press, 2015), 101.

138   *"We have to story"*: Tom Levitt, "Humanity Has Already Had Four Major Ecological Collapses: How Can We Avoid a Fifth," *Ecologist*, February 27, 2012.

140   *"we only protect"*: Tonino, Leath, "We Only Protect What We Love: Michael Soule on the Vanishing Wilderness," *Sun*, April 2018.

147 *"If people love you"*: Charles Eisenstein, "Amazon Rainforest Fires—Avoid This Trap," YouTube, August 23, 2019, https://www.youtube.com/watch?v=2mNboLb2Suc.

Chapter 11

150 *"The shortest distance"*: Anthony De Mello, *One Minute Wisdom* (New York: Doubleday, 1988), 23.
155 *"There must always be"*: W. H. Auden, *The Arts To-Day*, ed. Geoffrey Grigson (Port Washington, WI: Kennikat Press, 1970), 20.
157 *"We live by stories"*: Ben Okri, *A Way of Being Free* (London: Phoenix House, 1997), 46.

Chapter 12

169 *"A map without utopia"*: Oscar Wilde, *The Soul of Man under Socialism* (London: Arthur L. Humphreys, 1912), 43.
170 *"how people make Choices"*: The Leading Change Network, "Organizing Course—Week 2: Telling Your Public Story," YouTube, November 17, 2014, https://www.youtube.com/watch?v=S31LgV0sNqU.
170 *"What is this thing"*: Arundhati Roy, "Arundhati Roy: 'The Pandemic Is a Portal' | Free to Read," Financial Times, April 3, 2020, www.ft.com.
174 *"Buddhist teacher Pema Chödrön"*: Oprah Winfrey Network, "The Exercise That Could Help You Transcend Resentment," YouTube, October 20, 2019, https://www.youtube.com/watch?v=vN6hTFfqgd0.
178 *"If we didn't believe"*: W. S. Merwin, "Remembering Pulitzer Prize–Winning Poet W. S. Merwin," interview by Terri Gross, *Fresh Air*, June 13, 2008.